FEAR
in DOGS

Theories, protocols and solutions

anxiety
phobias
fight
flight
stress
reactive
defensive
triggers
environment
alert
threat
mistrust

Lynda Taylor MSc

'A complete and easy-to-use resource...I love, love, love this book!'
Leslie McDevitt

This book is dedicated to:

The fearful dogs who constantly help me to consider how my theoretical knowledge can be applied and adjusted for 'real world' application.

The rescue organisations who take on dogs with immense fears and who don't hesitate for a second to offer them time, space and an opportunity for a second chance in life.

The owners who offer up their homes to these broken souls and then spend weeks, months and years in gaining their trust to show them that humans can be a positive influence in their lives.

Acknowledgements

I would like to thank the amazingly talented and knowledgeable people who have guided my thinking over the years:

John Fisher – I had the immense fortune to meet and spend time with John early on in my career, and he started me on my journey into considering what was happening in the dog's mind.

To Susan G. Friedman, PhD, Ken Ramirez and Karen Pryor – who continue to motivate me, and to develop my understanding of animal behaviour..

My parents – who have never flinched or questioned my continual career changes, nor the latest life-changing plan or idea.

David, my partner – who is my biggest advocate, promoter, and motivator in encouraging me out of my comfort zone.

To our current gang of dogs:
Ellie, our working line Bearded Collie, whose speed of learning and insatiable enthusiasm makes me look so good as a trainer.

Reg, our former stray, whose independent character brings me right back down to size.

Fizz, who brings daily challenges and celebrations that come from living with a fearful dog.

Copyright © 2020 by Lynda Taylor and First Stone Publishing

First published in 2020 by First Stone Publishing, an imprint of Westline Publishing Limited

The Old Hen House, St Martin's Farm, Zeals, Warminster BA12 6NZ United Kingdom.

ISBN 9781910488591

Cover and interior design: Alan Cooper

Printed by Printworks Global, London/Hong Kong

1 2 3 4 5 6 7 8 9 0

CONTENTS

INTRODUCTION

When you have become used to living with confident dogs who quickly bounce back from new experiences, it can be tough to imagine the enormous impact that a fearful dog can have on a family. Inviting friends over becomes so stressful that you begin to avoid having anyone visit. Worries about fireworks start months in advance and walks at 4 am become the norm in your attempt to avoid anyone, or anything, that might cause your dog to experience a panic attack.

I had worked with owners of fearful dogs for many years, but it was my move to Spain, and subsequent volunteering with the rescue organisation, Galgos del Sol, which reminded me of an area of behavioural work that I find both challenging and hugely rewarding. Those celebrations for a dog who, finally, after months of staying in a kennel and run, decides to venture out and run into the exercise area. The huge breakthrough when the intensely mistrustful long-term resident finally sees some benefit to human interaction, even if that's just through the touching of a cone and the subsequent reinforcement. While these might seem relatively minor and almost inconsequential events to the well socialised and cared for pet, for these dogs who have experienced tremendous fear at the hands of their former carers, they are immense demonstrations of trust.

And then, Fizz arrived. Although I had experienced life with a fearful dog in the past, and had worked with hundreds of fearful dogs, and their owners, nothing quite prepared me for a young dog who had already lost trust in people. From being a stray in Madrid, to capture and diagnosis of parvo, followed by a long recuperation period at the vet, this young Galgo/Podenco cross had little experience on which to base any positive impressions of people. And all through a period which we know to be critical for a puppy to form a positive opinion of the world.

Fizz was terrified of anyone new coming into the home. My apologies to all those visitors whose holidays with us involved creeping around the house, checking with me if they could move or not, and avoiding all eye contact with Fizz throughout their stay!

I experienced the challenges that can come from being your dog's advocate and insisting on how interactions should take place. To the vet who I told not to lift Fizz on to the scales but proceeded to do so, I hope your Crocs cleaned up okay from the flood of urine which Fizz directed into their holes! The squelching, as you walked back to the consulting room, shoes filled with warm urine, is a noise I will never forget...

I still wonder if people talk about that weird woman who, when out walking her dogs, would cross the road as they came close and then stop and watch them until they could no longer be seen. This was all because Fizz could not, initially, walk forward if he could see anyone other than my partner, or myself. Any attempt to walk on would see Fizz walking backwards, compelled to keep the stranger in sight, until they disappeared from view.

All those experiences, and more, have made me think about of how tough life can be for those owners who find themselves with a fearful dog in their family.

My aim for this book is to provide information on several levels:

For owners: there is accessible, and detailed, information, so they can understand what is happening without needing in-depth knowledge in learning theory or behavioural science.

For students enrolled on canine courses: there are clearly-written descriptions, and instructions, so that the techniques and approaches become easy to differentiate.

For those who want to dig deeper: research papers are referenced for further reading.

There are few absolutes when working with fearful dogs; what works well in one case may not have the same results in what seems to be a very similar situation. This means that while trainers and behaviourists need to have a toolbox of techniques, they also need to see the dog, and his family, as unique individuals.

I hope this book delivers a range of techniques, of which one might just provide the key in helping a fearful dog live a calmer and less stressful life.

1 THE PURPOSE OF FEAR

In this chapter, I look at how we define fear, its causes, and its purpose.

If a fearful dog is part of your family, this chapter will help you to recognise that their fear serves a purpose, and it may also provide some clues as to how the fear became established.

If you are a student, or looking for more in-depth detail on the purpose and origins of fear, I discuss several research papers for which the full details are provided at the end of the chapter.

Fear is an emotional response that can be seen in the physiological, and behavioural, reactions of a dog when something is perceived as being frightening or is a predictor of danger. It is an entirely normal reaction, and it plays a significant role in keeping our dogs safe. In fact, the fear seen during a puppy's fear period is a way of balancing his desire to investigate the environment while being kept safe from harm.

But when the fearful behaviour is out of proportion to the danger the threat poses, we need to look at ways of reducing the scale of the escalation. Reducing, rather than extinguishing, the fear is an important consideration, because in some situations there is value in showing a little caution. When meeting a new dog, for example, that caution may result in paying more attention to the other dog's body language. That, in turn, results in a calm, polite greeting, rather than bouncing right up without a care in the world and promptly being told where to go!

DEFINITIONS

The three terms – fear, anxiety and phobia – are often used interchangeably, even within research papers, but they do have three quite different meanings:

FEAR
Fear can be defined as an internal early warning system that issues a call to action. That means the response that takes place when something causes us either to defend ourselves or to run away. Fear is a normal, biological response to a genuine threat, and a fearful response can be learnt from situations where pain or stress is experienced. That, in turn, can result in avoidance behaviour should the dog find himself, once more, in that same situation. For example, the dog who was startled when you dropped a baking tray on to the floor, may become fearful of going back into the kitchen next time you're baking.

However, we should be aware that multiple factors influence whether fear is experienced. These include genes, development, cognition, behaviour, learning, physiology, and neuroanatomy. When we are working with a fearful dog, more than one of these factors will be in play, and that means that we will need a multi-faceted approach to our behaviour modification plan.

ANXIETY

Anxiety relates to an unpleasant, and vague, sense of apprehension. If you are walking down a dark street, you may feel a little uneasy because there is the possibility of a stranger jumping out from behind a bush. Your anxiety is not the result of a known or specific threat; instead, it comes from the mind's interpretation of what might happen. A sense of anxiety doesn't even need to relate to a known threat or a particular concern, and that vagueness is a strong contributor to how both we, and our dogs, can feel.

Experiencing a lack of control, in this way, contributes to the feelings of anxiety and that, in turn, makes coping more difficult. It is mainly based on the potential for future threats or danger, or even upcoming, potentially negative events. Anxiety disorders result in overestimating the likelihood of threat. The same biological reactions that are experienced with fear are taking place but, this time, with the absence of a trigger. So, the person who is worried about walking down a dark street may grossly overestimate the likelihood of being attacked. This then results in increased levels of anxiety, which trigger a self-protective response. The autonomic system kicks in with its fight or flight response, so the body is ready to react should something happen. The physical symptoms – the increase in heart rate and rapid breathing – provide yet more evidence.

For an anxious dog, the situation is just the same: his body prepares him for a perceived attack, even though there may be little evidence that one is about to happen.

PHOBIAS

Phobias are also defensive behaviours to protect against harm, even when it would seem that they are irrational. In just the same way as a fear, they are deeply wired into the autonomic nervous system as a legitimate response to help the individual survive. So, even when a dog's phobia of thunder seems to be irrelevant to survival, the perceived lack of damage following his response is considered to be a positive outcome and justifies the response.

A fear is classified as a phobia when the response to a stimulus becomes increasingly extreme, or irrational, in nature. It would be reasonable for a dog to get a fright when there is a sudden and loud clap of thunder; for the phobic dog, the response might be intense shaking, urinating or defecating in the home, or trying to escape.

CAUSES OF FEAR

It is not always necessary to know how the problem started to help the fearful dog. However, having an awareness of the causes of fear can help to guard against the problem becoming worse or prevent fear occurring in the first place.

They can be categorised as follows:

ENVIRONMENTAL FEAR

While both physiology and development will influence a dog's behaviour, it is their current environment that triggers the fearful response. This could be the arrival of a stranger at the door, seeing a particular type of dog, which has attacked in the past, or a loud clap of thunder.

That trigger may also have a range of criteria around it, which either allows the dog to continue with a minimal emotional response or to become fearful. For example, consider a dog with a fear of men wearing hats:

- At a distance of 6m (20ft) the dog shows signs of becoming aware of the trigger in his environment but he is still able to respond to requests from his owner and eat a treat.
- At 3m (10ft) the dog may show signs of fear in his body language and, though able to respond to requests, he is distracted, reluctant to eat a treat, and very focused on the trigger.
- At 1.5m (5ft) the dog is overcome by fear and is no longer able to respond to requests from his owner, or even consider eating.

While we may consider 6m to be the point at which the trigger begins to cause signs of fear, we should be aware that these are the signs we notice. There may be more subtle indications we have missed, or processing information relating to the trigger has just started within the sympathetic nervous system, which may have been triggered at a distance of 9m.

BEHAVIOUR OF OTHERS

The escalation, or diminishing effects of a fearful situation, can depend on the responses of those around the dog. The man in the hat, from the previous example, may continue on his way, paying little attention to the dog who, in turn, expresses only very low levels of fear. However, if that same hat-wearing man decides to 'help' by coming and saying hello to the dog, the fear expressed may escalate.

Let us imagine you are out for a walk with your dog, when another dog, the imposter, appears from nowhere and begins to act aggressively. Three scenarios can then play out:

1. Your dog communicates a 'no threat' signal through his body language.

That message is received and acknowledged by the imposter so the situation may de-escalate.

2. If the fright causes your dog to escalate his behaviour, it may well cause the same response in the imposter.

3. If your dog escalates, the imposter may switch to showing 'no threat' body language and de-escalate the situation.

In each one of these scenarios, your dog is learning about the outcomes of his behavioural responses. Do be aware, though, his definition of a good outcome may be different to yours!

Let us now consider how our reactions may influence the situation. It can be tough having a fearful dog, especially when it was never your intention to be in that situation, as opposed to adopting a dog with known fear issues. Thinking about the previous scenario – a surprise encounter with another dog – we also have choices in how we react. However, unless we plan for these situations and have a clear understanding of what we should do, our sympathetic, fight/flight system can take over, in just the same way as happens with our dogs.

For ideas and strategies to help you plan for these types of situations, see *Chapter Four: Welcoming a Fearful Dog into your home and Chapter Five: Assessing and Working with Fearful Dogs.*

FACTORS BEFORE BIRTH

While we tend to think of fear as something that has developed with experience, there are other factors that can increase the likelihood of it becoming a problem. There is growing evidence that the environment within the uterus (intrauterine) has an important role in shaping foetal development, resulting in long-term behavioural implications.

We know that, during the development of the foetus, an adequate energy and protein supply, along with essential fatty acids, and various key micro-nutrients, are all required to supply the necessary substrates for foetal tissue development within the central nervous system. We also know that they are needed within the biochemical processes that coordinate healthy brain development.

Although the transplacental transfer of cortisol has not been studied in dogs, it has been researched in both rats and humans (Glover, 2015). When the mother of the pups is placed in a high-stress situation, it can result in the foetuses receiving cortisol to help prepare them for the stressful environment. However, this comes at a cost, as the pups, once born, are more likely to be both reactive and fearful.

This does not mean that the mother needs to be overly cosseted because we also know, from human studies, that a moderate amount of stress during pregnancy leads to a child who is more adept at tasks requiring reasoning and coordination (Grace et al. 2005). We should, however, be conscious of any situations that the dam finds very stressful, such as fireworks, and avoid exposure to them during her pregnancy.

FACTORS FROM BIRTH AND DURING PUPPYHOOD

Birth Factors

Puppies that have been hand-reared, orphaned or born by Caesarean section and subsequently rejected by their mothers, have been found to develop behavioural issues that are associated with anxiety and fear (Jagoe, 1994). While this isn't a certainty, it's something that rescue centres, breeders and owners should be aware of in order to plan effective socialisation opportunities and the introduction of new environments.

PUPPYHOOD

1-3 weeks of age

Research conducted by Gazzano and his team, in 2008, identified the positive impact that came from the daily gentle handling of puppies. They found that handling or 'gentling', when carried out from the third day following birth through to day 21, had a positive influence on the pups' emotional development. When the puppies were assessed at eight weeks of age, by being placed in isolation for three minutes, they found

that the handled pups were calmer than those who had not been handled. They also found that when the puppies were individually placed in a larger area with novel objects, such as toys, the handled pups explored their environment more than the non-handled pups.

3-5 weeks of age

As the pups develop and reach the 3-5-week stage, they are beginning to explore their environment. At around this age, they are in a period of parasympathetic dominance, which means they experience all the factors associated with being relaxed, such as a low heart rate. This then creates the perfect environment for a youngster to investigate both new and familiar objects with equal curiosity and to begin to store memories resulting from his explorations.

Slowly the puppy begins to evaluate his surroundings through making comparisons with the memories already formed. To increase the likelihood of the puppy accepting new experiences, without becoming fearful, he needs to be exposed to a wide range of stimuli, and new environments, to develop a bank of memories that can be referenced in the future.

5-7 weeks of age

That 'natural, relaxed frame of mind' is now replaced by a period of high heart rate as the sympathetic flight/ fight system takes hold until the puppy is around eight weeks of age. When the puppy encounters new things, and he has missed out on forming a positive response to them in the previous stage, they are now more likely to trigger a fearful reaction. That doesn't mean to say that he will stop exploring; he will still be drawn towards investigating new things as long as he is provided with the opportunity to do so at his own pace. This experience then adds to his bank of positive experiences. However, if he is pressured to approach, the opposite effect is likely to be seen in the form of fear or anxiety. This, in turn, results in the development of a negative association.

After seven weeks

At this point, much of the puppy's view of the world is formed. While on-going socialisation and habituation will build his memory bank, those early experiences play a crucial part in whether he investigates with curiosity, or backs away in fear.

Research, carried out in 2002 by Appleby, Bradshaw and Casey, found that there is a connection between the development of fear-related behaviours and the dog's early environment. Those dogs who had spent their first weeks in a home environment with a breeder and then, after vaccinations, experienced urban life, had a reduced likelihood of developing avoidance behaviour or aggression towards strangers. Sadly, for those dogs who had been reared in a non-home environment, such as a

barn or shed, there was an increased likelihood of aggressive behaviour when examined by a vet.

It is important to appreciate that not every dog raised in a kennel environment will end up being fearful and, equally, events may occur that cause a carefully raised pup to become fearful. However, if you are looking to improve your odds of having a confident adult dog, you should ensure that pups who are raised in a kennel environment go on to have a wide range of appropriate socialisation and habituation opportunities.

THE SENIOR DOG

Behavioural changes can be one of the first signs in the declining wellbeing of an older dog. However, it is important that assessments are carried out to differentiate between what might be expected with normal ageing, and indications that there may be other factors in play.

Dogs over the age of eight years old may experience a neurobehavioural syndrome, which is known as canine cognitive dysfunction or CDS. This is the result of changes in the structure of the brain that can then lead to changes in behaviour. There are several signs that CDS may be present, and this includes signs of disorientation, decreasing social interactions and increased anxiety. There are some indications from research (Milgram, 2005) that enrichment, in the form of physical exercise, social interactions, and cognitive activities, can preserve, and actually improve, the brain function in old dogs. However, we should bear in mind that these studies were undertaken within laboratory settings where the opportunities for enrichment may have been low before the research started. It is not clear if the same results would be found for dogs who already had a history of living in a stimulating environment.

One important message for senior dog owners is to keep on training! Lifelong learning does seem to delay the ageing of attentional capture, sustained attention, and selective attention in pet dogs of various breeds (Chapagain et al., 2017).

EMOTIONAL STATE BEFORE THE TRIGGER

We also need to consider how our dog's emotional state, before the trigger, may influence the ease with which it causes a fearful response.

We know that the recovery period from experiencing fear to returning to a state of calmness can vary enormously from dog to dog. We also know that the recovery period will be influenced by the intensity of the fear response and also how the situation was managed by the owner who may, inadvertently, intensify the response through their actions.

Trigger stacking can be viewed as 'the straw that breaks the camel's back'. A build-up of relatively minor stresses can combine to give a response that seems to be out of proportion to the situation. For more information on trigger stacking, see *Chapter 8: Habituation*.

Research papers:

Appleby, D.L., Bradshaw, J.W. and Casey, R.A. (2002) 'Relationship between aggressive and avoidance behaviour by dogs and their experience in the first six months of life.' Veterinary Record 150, pp. 434–438.

Chapagain, D., Virányi, Z., Wallis, L.J., Huber, L., Serra, J.and Range,F. (2017) 'Aging of attentiveness in border collies and other pet dog breeds: the protective benefits of lifelong training.' Frontiers in Aging Neuroscience 9(100).

Gazzano, A., Mariti, C., Notari, L., Sighieri, C. and McBride, A.E. (2008) 'Effects of early gentling and early environment on emotional development of puppies.' Applied Animal Behaviour Science 110, pp. 294–304.

Glover, V. (2015) 'Prenatal stress and its effects on the fetus and the child: possible underlying biological mechanisms.' In Perinatal Programming of Neurodevelopment. Springer, New York, NY: pp. 269-283

Grace, T., Bulsara, M., Robinson, M. and Hands, B. (2005) *The Impact of Maternal Gestational Stress on Motor Development in Late Childhood and Adolescence: A Longitudinal Study.* Child Development, 87(1)

Jagoe, J.A. (1994) *'Behaviour problems in the Domestic Dog: A retrospective and prospective study to identify factors influencing their development.'* Unpublished PhD Thesis. University of Cambridge. Reported In: Serpell, J. A. and Jagoe, J. A. (1995) Chapter 6: Early experience and the development of behaviour. In: Serpell, J. (Ed) The Domestic Dog – its Evolution, Behaviour.

Milgram, N. (2005) *'Learning ability in aged beagle dogs is preserved by behavioral enrichment and dietary fortification: a two-year longitudinal study.'* Neurobiology of Aging, 26, pp. 77–90.

Storengen, L. M. and Lingaas, F. (2015) *'Noise sensitivity in 17 breeds: Prevalence, breed risk and correlation with fear in other situations.'* Applied Animal Behaviour Science, 171, pp. 152-160.

Weinstock, M. (2005) *'The potential influence of maternal stress hormones on development and mental health of the offspring.'* Brain, Behavior, and Immunity. 19(4) pp. 296-308.

This chapter provides an overview of the key structures involved in the processing of fear responses before going into more detail about how neurotransmitters can influence behaviour. It concludes with details of research into the physiology of fear for those of you who would like to dig a little deeper into this fascinating topic!

When we are working with fearful dogs, we tend to focus on the output of their brain rather than the mechanics of what is going on inside them. While we may not need to know the intricacies of neurological processing, some background knowledge can be very useful.

There is a growing school of thought that advocates psychopharmacological as a first line of action rather than a last resort, so it is becoming even more important to understand how the brain works, and how these medications affect the way it processes information.

THE NERVOUS SYSTEM

A dog's body is unable to operate without the nervous system – a complex network that coordinates his actions, reflexes, and sensations. The nervous system is organised into two key parts, the central nervous system (CNS) and the peripheral nervous system (PNS).

CENTRAL NERVOUS SYSTEM (CNS)

The central nervous system is the body's processing centre and is made up of the brain and the spinal cord. Within these, there is both grey matter and white matter.

Grey matter comprises neuron cell bodies, their dendrites, glial cells, synapses and capillaries.

- **Neurons** are the cells within the nervous system that transmit information to other nerve cells, muscle, or gland cells.
- **Dendrites** extend from the neuron cell body and receive messages from other neurons.
- **Glia cells** don't carry nerve impulses, but they do have many essential functions in allowing the neurons to function correctly.
- **Synapses** are the structures that allow a neuron (or nerve cell) to pass an electrical or chemical signal to another neuron or the target effector cell.
- **Capillaries** are the tiny blood vessels that help to connect arteries and veins, along with facilitating the exchange of elements between blood and tissues. In the brain, the continuous capillaries

are part of the blood-brain barrier, which helps to protect the brain by only allowing essential nutrients to cross.

White matter refers to the areas of the CNS that host the majority of axons, the long cords that extend from neurons and take information away from the cell body. Most axons are coated in myelin – a white, fatty, insulating cover – that helps nerve signals travel quickly and reliably.

ANATOMY OF THE BRAIN

The brain is the command centre for the nervous system. It receives signals from the body's sensory organs and outputs information to the muscles.

The dog's brain has the same basic structure as all other mammal brains, though when compared to a human brain it is smaller in relation to body size.

It consists of:

Hindbrain: This consists of the brainstem, which connects the brain to the spinal cord, and the cerebellum. The brainstem is made up of:

- **Medulla oblongata:** This is responsible for respiratory and cardiac function.
- **Cranial nerves:** These pass through the medulla to transmit information from the head and the neck to the spinal cord.

- **Pons:** This is a bridge between various parts of the nervous system, including the cerebellum and cerebrum. Many vital nerves originate in the pons, including the trigeminal nerve responsible for feeling in the face, chewing and swallowing. It also stimulates and controls the intensity of breathing and has been associated with the control of sleep cycles.
- **Cerebellum (meaning little brain in Latin):** This is involved in coordination. It is now becoming apparent that it plays a critical role in creating fluidity between thoughts, actions, emotions, and social interactions.

Midbrain: This area of the brain is primarily associated with visual reflexes and reactions to moving stimuli. It is also involved in arousal and attention and, interestingly, from the trainer's perspective, behaviours that are controlled by rewards. Additionally, structures within the midbrain are important for organising behaviours such as predatory and defensive aggression.

Forebrain: By far the largest region of the brain, the forebrain contains the cerebrum and several other structures nestled within it: the thalamus, the hypothalamus, the pineal gland and the limbic system.

Cerebrum or cerebral cortex: This is where most of the key brain functions take place, including receiving and analysing information related to thinking, interpreting and processing sensory inputs, pain, and vision. The cerebral cortex is divided into two areas: the left and right cerebral hemispheres. Within these two areas are four lobes: frontal, temporal, parietal and occipital.

1. **Frontal lobe**: Although not as developed in dogs as it is in humans, this is where many outputs associated with behaviour commence, including general alertness, intelligence, and the temperament of each individual.
2. **Temporal lobe:** Concerned with learning and memory, the temporal lobe is where the limbic system can be found. This area comprises the hippocampus, which is involved with learning, spatial memory and stress responses, and the amygdala, which prepares the body for an emergency or a fear-inducing situation. This area also stores memories relating to fear and emotional events for future reference.
3. **Parietal lobe:** This area receives information from the body and head, including that relating to pain and the position of limbs. It is also responsible for cognition and selective attention.
4. **Occipital lobe:** This lobe allows the dog to see and process stimuli from the external world.

Basal Ganglia

This group of nuclei are located deep within the brain and are best known for their role in controlling movement. The basal ganglia facilitates wanted behaviours and stops unwanted behaviours. As with many parts of the brain, we tend to learn their purpose when things go wrong. So, that means when it's not functioning correctly, it can result in unwanted, involuntary movement.

In addition to the motor cortex, the basal ganglia also forms loops with the prefrontal cortex. Because the prefrontal cortex is involved in planning, thinking, and awareness, the basal ganglia may also be responsible for facilitating wanted thoughts and stopping unwanted thoughts. Hence, it is believed to possess functions associated with obsessive-compulsive disorder, depression, and dementia.

PERIPHERAL NERVOUS SYSTEM (PNS)

Everything else, aside from the brain and spinal cord, sits within the peripheral nervous system. This, in turn, is divided into two systems: the somatic nervous system and the autonomic nervous system.

The **somatic nervous system** is responsible for the movement of voluntary muscles and the reflex arc, a neural pathway that controls a reflexive response, such as pulling your hand away from something hot. The system carries nerve impulses back and forth between the central nervous system and the skeletal muscles, skin, and sensory organs.

The **autonomic nervous system** regulates bodily functions, such as heart rate, digestion, and respiratory rate. It is made up of two antagonistic sets of nerves: the sympathetic and parasympathetic nervous systems.

The **sympathetic nervous system** connects the internal organs to the brain by spinal nerves. When a stressful situation stimulates the 'fight or flight' response, these nerves prepare the organism by increasing the heart rate, increasing blood flow to the muscles, and decreasing blood flow to the skin.

The **parasympathetic nervous system** has almost the exact opposite effect of the sympathetic system in that it relaxes the body and inhibits, or slows, many high-energy functions.

NEUROTRANSMITTERS

Neurotransmitters are the chemical messengers of the body. Their role is to transmit signals from nerve cells to specific receptors on target cells, which may be in muscles, glands, or other nerves. Each neurotransmitter attaches to a different receptor so that means, for example, that the dopamine molecules attach to dopamine receptors. When they attach, it causes a response in the target cells. Once the neurotransmitters have delivered their messages, the body either recycles or breaks them down

KEY NEUROTRANSMITTERS

Neurotransmitters have several different types of action which include:

- Excitatory neurotransmitters: Encourage a target cell to take action.
- Inhibitory neurotransmitters: Decrease the chances of the target cell taking action and may have a relaxation-like effect.
- Modulatory neurotransmitters: Send messages to several neurons at the same time and also communicate with other neurotransmitters.

Some of the best-known neurotransmitters include the following:

Acetylcholine (Ach)

This is an excitatory neurotransmitter that triggers muscle contractions. It also controls the heartbeat and stimulates some hormones. Ach also plays an important role in brain function and memory.

Low levels of acetylcholine are linked to issues with memory and thinking, such as memory loss. In contrast, high levels of acetylcholine can cause excessive muscle contraction, which can lead to seizures, spasms, and other health issues.

Ach binds to two different receptor types: nicotinic and muscarinic. *Nicotinic* receptors are believed to cause other neurotransmitters to be released, resulting in a range of different effects.

Muscarinic receptors are associated with forming memories, learning and movement.

Dopamine (DA)

This is often known as the pleasure or reward neurotransmitter, as it is released by the brain when taking part in enjoyable activities. Dopamine is important for memory, learning, behaviour, and movement coordination. The dopamine system is especially sensitive to cues that a reward is coming, so that means that when that cue is attended to, it sets off the dopamine system. So, interestingly, it is not necessarily the reward itself that keeps the dopamine loop going; it could be the anticipation of the reward.

When there is a deficiency in dopamine, there can be an inability to learn, anxiety and irritability. If there is too much dopamine, you may see impulsivity, agitation and reactivity.

It is thought that diet may help to balance dopamine levels, as amino acids – found in protein-rich food – are needed to produce it. It is also suggested that saturated fat, and a deficiency in vitamin D, can lower dopamine activity. While there are no dopamine supplements, exercise may naturally boost the levels of this neurotransmitter.

Norepinephrine/epinephrine

Also known as noradrenaline and adrenaline, norepinephrine and epinephrine act as both neurotransmitters and hormones. They have similar chemical structures, but they produce different effects on the body.

When the brain perceives danger, the amygdala triggers the hypothalamus to activate the autonomic nervous system. This stimulates the adrenal gland to start releasing epinephrine into the bloodstream. This rush of epinephrine is involved in the fight/flight response and so can be released as a response to being stressed or scared. As a result, there is an increase in heart and breathing rate, and the brain is also primed to make quick decisions.

The adrenal medulla produces norepinephrine in response to low blood pressure and stress. This results in the narrowing of the blood vessels, meaning that there is an increase in blood pressure. Like epinephrine, norepinephrine also increases the heart rate and blood sugar levels.

Low levels of epinephrine and norepinephrine can result in a number of physical and mental symptoms, including anxiety, depression, problems sleeping and low blood sugar. In addition, norepinephrine plays a role in focus and promotes periods of sustained attention. Low levels of norepinephrine may result in difficulties with attention, concentration and decreased cognitive ability.

Serotonin

Serotonin is the key hormone that stabilises mood along with feelings of wellbeing, and happiness. It also has a broader effect on the body in that it enables brain cells, and other nervous system cells, to communicate with each other. It also helps with sleep, eating, and digestion.

When serotonin levels become low, it can result in impulsive and aggressive behaviour, impaired learning, anxiety and obsessive behaviour. Too much serotonin, on the other hand, can cause shivering, muscle rigidity, fever and seizures.

There is some evidence that serotonin levels may be increased via exposure to sunlight and through vigorous exercise. Dietary amino acids, including tryptophan, have been shown to have an effect on serotonin function. However, mammals are unable to synthesise tryptophan, which means that levels in the brain are dependent upon its concentration within the diet.

For a while, feeding turkey, with its reportedly high level of tryptophan, was promoted as a way of increasing serotonin and, as a result, providing a calming effect on anxious dogs. However, there were three key flaws with this theory:

Firstly, a high tryptophan meal is unable to cause significant changes in serotonin levels in the blood or the synapses of neurons.

Secondly, to be converted into serotonin, tryptophan must cross the blood-brain barrier to enter the brain. However, this barrier is very selective and only accepts a certain number of amino acids of each type. While tryptophan does increase in the blood after a protein-rich meal, its very large molecules are competing with several other similar types of amino acids. This then means that only a very limited amount of tryptophan makes it into the brain for conversion.

Finally, turkey meat does not actually contain a uniquely high level of tryptophan. It is similar to the levels found in other meats and has only half the concentration found in some plant-sourced proteins.

Calming diets have now been formulated which are designed to provide tryptophan with a competitive edge across the blood brain barrier, which then results in an increased level of serotonin.

THE ENDOCRINE SYSTEM

The endocrine system is a series of glands that produce, and secrete, hormones that the body then uses for a wide range of functions. Some neurotransmitters, such as norepinephrine and epinephrine, are also hormones, which we have already discussed (see page 18), but there are a number of other hormones that influence behaviour:

CORTISOL

Often known as the stress hormone, cortisol is a steroid hormone produced by the adrenal glands. It does have other roles: it manages how the body uses carbohydrates, fats, and proteins, keeps inflammation down, regulates blood pressure and controls the sleep/wake cycle. Cortisol receptors are in most cells of the body, and when the body is on high alert, cortisol can alter or shut down functions that get in the way. That includes digestive and reproductive systems, the immune system and growth processes.

For cortisol to come into play, a multi-step process needs to be undertaken:

1. The amygdala has to recognise that there is a threat.
2. The amygdala sends a message to the hypothalamus, which releases corticotropin-releasing hormone (CRH).
3. CRH tells the pituitary gland to release adrenocorticotropic hormone (ACTH).
4. ACTH tells the adrenal glands to produce cortisol.

Once released, cortisol takes action by:

• Preparing the body for a fight-or-flight response by flooding it with glucose, which provides an immediate energy source for the large muscles.
• Inhibiting the production of insulin to prevent the glucose from being stored and, instead, promoting its immediate use.
• Narrowing the arteries while the epinephrine increases heart rate, both of which force blood to pump harder and faster.

When a dog is consistently in a fight/flight situation, such as he may experience in a kennel environment, heightened levels of cortisol may be circulating in his body. This, in turn, weakens the immune system, leaving his body vulnerable to diseases and infection.

Testosterone

Testosterone increases the production of noradrenaline and arginine vasopressin resulting in an increase in risk-taking behaviours and the reduction of fear. Castration in male dogs removes the main site for the production of testosterone. There is some testosterone production within the adrenal cortex, but it is generally considered to be of quite insignificant levels.

With the removal of testosterone comes the removal of the confidence and fear inhibition it provided. This, in turn, may increase fear-related behaviours. Testosterone is also known to increase serotonin, and so its removal may also reduce its known calming effect.

The potential benefits of castration, and consideration of how existing fear may be impacted, need to be balanced with great care.

Vasopressin

Also known as the antidiuretic hormone (ADH), vasopressin has a number of different roles in controlling various bodily functions. There has recently also been a number of studies looking at the connection of this hormone with canine fear responses. Two of these studies have been included in the research section (see below).

Research papers

Dreschel, N.A. (2010). *'The effects of fear and anxiety on health and lifespan in pet dogs.'* Applied Animal Behavior Science, 125 (3-4).

Dreschel considered that stress responses are related to a number of physiological changes in the dog's body which, in many species, are related to disease and shortened lifespan.

A total of 721 owners of deceased dogs completed a 99-point questionnaire, which gathered information on demographics, training, behavioural characteristics, health history, age at, and cause, of death in their pets.

She found that dogs with extreme non-social fear and separation anxiety had an increased severity and frequency of skin disorders, and that fear of strangers related to a significantly shortened lifespan.

Dreschel, N. A. and Grange, D.A. (2005). *'Physiological and behavioural reactivity to stress.'* Applied Animal Behavior Science, 95.

This research looked at the interactions between hypothalamic–pituitary–adrenal (HPA) axis activation in response to stress, relationship quality, and behaviour in thunderstorm-anxious dogs and their owners. Traditionally, the HPA axis has been seen as the body's stress system which controls levels of cortisol and other important stress-related hormones.

Working with dogs in their homes, Dreschel and Granger manipulated exposure to thunder, which was known to be a highly feared stressor. They then assessed both the dogs' and their caregivers' physiological and behavioural responsiveness. They did this by taking saliva samples from 19 dog–owner pairs before exposure to a recording of a thunderstorm, and then again 20 minutes, and 40 minutes after exposure to the recording. Using these samples, the cortisol levels could then be measured.

Focusing on the results from the dogs, they saw signs of fear, which included pacing, whining and hiding, and they also found that their cortisol levels increased by 207 per cent. After a time lapse of 40 minutes, it had still not returned to the level prior to the thunderstorm sounds. Interestingly, the presence of other dogs in the household was linked to less reactivity and a more rapid recovery of the dog's HPA response.

Katoe, M., Miyaji, K., Nobuyo, O. and Mitsuaki, O. (2012). *'Effects of prescription diet on dealing with stressful situations and performance of anxiety-related behaviors in privately owned anxious dogs.'* Journal of Veterinary Behavior, 7 21-26.

The researchers decided to evaluate the effects of a diet, which had been supplemented with alpha-casozepine and L-tryptophan, on the stress response of anxious dogs. A total of 44 privately owned dogs took part in the research. First of all, they were fed the control diet, followed by the study diet, each for an eight-week period, with a transitional period of one week between each.

After seven weeks on a particular diet, the owners were asked to report on their dogs' behaviour by filling out a questionnaire. Interestingly, the effect of the study diet was found to be significant for four anxiety-related behavioural parameters, which might show a placebo effect.

After seven weeks on each diet, the urine cortisol-to-creatinine ratio (UCCR) was measured to assess the stress response to a visit to a veterinary practice for nail clipping. They found that the stressor-induced increase was significantly lower in the dogs when they were fed the study diet than earlier when they were fed the control diet. The study diet seemed to improve the ability of an individual to cope with stress and may reduce anxiety-related behaviour in anxious dogs.

Pirrone, F., Pierantoni, L., Bossetti, A., Uccheddo, S. and Albertini, M. (2019). *'Salivary Vasopressin as a Potential Non–Invasive Biomarker of Anxiety in Dogs Diagnosed with Separation–Related Problems.'* Animals 9 (12).

In this study, the researchers analysed the salivary fluctuations in both behaviourally normal dogs and dogs with separation distress following a three-minute separation from their owner, within a new environment. They found that dogs with a previous diagnosis of separation distress showed more anxiety-related behaviours and higher concentrations of vasopressin than control dogs when separated from their owners.

MacLean, E.L., Gesquiere, L.R., Gruen, M.E., Sherman, B.I., Martin, L. and Carter, C.S. (2017). *'Endogenous Oxytocin, Vasopressin, and Aggression in Domestic Dogs.'* Frontiers in Psychology. 8.

This team of researchers investigated the relationships between oxytocin and vasopressin and aggression in domestic dogs. Focusing on the vasopressin results, they found that dogs with a history of aggression exhibited more aggressive behaviour during simulated encounters with other dogs and had higher total vasopressin than the control group.

The researchers then went on to compare the vasopressin concentrations between pet dogs and a population of assistance dogs that have been bred for affiliative and non-aggressive temperaments. Compared to pet dogs, there were no differences in the vasopressin levels. However, within the assistance dogs, who behaved more aggressively toward a threatening stranger, there was a higher concentration of vasopressin compared with dogs who did not react.

So often we focus solely on the dog and the problems he is presenting, whether that relates to helping your own fearful dog, or working with a client. However, the human factor in assisting fearful dogs is so significant that it warrants its own chapter in this book.

Every interaction that an owner has with their fearful dog can build trust and understanding, or it can undermine the relationship. But, when it undermines, it needs to be recognised that those actions are often not the result of intentional, considered decisions. There are often many reasons why, despite an apparent desire on the owner's part to help their dog overcome his fears, the problem just doesn't seem to get any smaller.

As a behaviourist helping a client, that lack of progress is frustrating and can, at times, cause self-doubt. As an owner, it can lead to a sense of despair and concern as to whether they can offer this dog the home that he needs.

Within this chapter, I will be discussing some of the human psychological theories, which can explain why progress with a fearful dog may not go to plan. If you are reading this chapter as a behaviourist, it will provide you with the understanding that the lack of progress may not be down to your misguided advice, or the client not 'putting in the time'. In turn, it will hopefully allow you to look at the human factors from a science-based approach; much the same as you do when you consider the fearful dog.

If you are reading as the owner of a fearful dog, I hope that this chapter will provide you with an awareness that our best intentions can be sabotaged by the ways in which our brains cope with, and interpret, situations. Once we are aware of what might be happening, we can change our strategy and move forward.

UNDERSTANDING THE ISSUE

The Dunning Kruger Effect

The Dunning-Kruger effect, coined by the psychologists David Dunning and Justin Kruger in 1999, is a cognitive bias in which poor performers greatly over-estimate their abilities. A cognitive bias is caused by errors in our thinking. These happen when we are processing, and interpreting, information in the world around us. Our mistaken conclusions then go on to affect the decisions and judgments that we make.

These biases might mean that we are

drawn to information that confirms the beliefs we already have, and we then ignore details that contradict them. For example, we might be firm in our belief that a particular approach to helping a fearful dog is the right one, and we actively look for evidence that confirms our decision. When we come across opinions that suggest there are some downsides to that approach, we ignore them.

Dunning and Kruger's research showed that there is a cognitive bias in which under-performing individuals "reach erroneous conclusions, and make unfortunate choices, but their incompetence robs them of the ability to realise it". This incompetence, in turn, leads them to "inflated views of their performance and ability". So, that can mean that we blame a technique for not working when perhaps it was the wrong choice, or that it was applied incorrectly. But rather than developing the underpinning knowledge of how that technique works, or putting in the time to perfect the skills it requires, we blame the process as being ineffective.

Have you ever been in that situation that the more that you know, the more you realise how much you don't know? I definitely had those moments when I was studying for my MSc in Applied Animal Behaviour and Training. The more I researched and the deeper I delved into the science of why animals behave in a particular way, along with

intricate details of the training process, then another door would open, ready to swallow up any preconceptions I had held of my level of knowledge!

With the door open, we have a choice. We can either step through the doorway and begin the next chapter of our learning journey. Or, we can step back, close the door and stay in our comfort zone, along with our cognitive biases. As a lecturer, I have frequently seen students close the door behind them when they received a grade that was lower than expected. It was easier to leave the course than face the possibility that their knowledge was not where they thought it to be. Changing the perceptions we hold of ourselves is not easy; I have, therefore, covered this subject in more detail (see Belief structures, page 33).

A skilled animal behaviourist takes on the role of a detective. They look at the problem from all angles; they consider a wide range of options and then begin to shortlist potential solutions, all the time assessing the strengths and weaknesses of their strategy. They also know that every case is different; what works for one dog with a fear of the vet, for example, may not be appropriate for another dog presenting similar fearful responses.

With this constant process of reflection and evaluation, we can avoid falling prey to the Dunning-Kruger effect. We need to honestly, and routinely, question our knowledge, and the conclusions we make, rather than blindly accepting them. David Dunning suggests that we should be our own devil's advocate by challenging ourselves to probe how we might possibly be wrong. In doing so, we may find that our approach or assumptions were correct, but we now have the evidence to substantiate that decision.

The issue with the Dunning-Kruger effect is that we may not realise when we are within its grasp.

It may sound pretty obvious to state: "we don't know, what we don't know". However, when we fail to question our approaches to helping fearful dogs objectively, and do not commit to an ethos of continually developing our knowledge, then the chances are we are heading down that slippery slope.

Equally, we should recognise that this is not a deliberate, preconceived plan to make poor decisions. So, just as we would not get cross or frustrated at a dog who doesn't yet understand a cue, we also need to approach these situations with an appreciation of the psychology that underpins them.

There are two key ways that we can ensure that we maintain an informed understanding of our abilities:

Firstly, we can seek out others whose

expertise can help cover our blind spots, such as turning to a colleague, or professional, for advice or constructive criticism. This is harder if you are working with your own dog, as it can be tough to accurately assess what is happening and to consider how your own behaviour and beliefs are actually holding back progress. This is why it can be so helpful to have the assistance of someone outside of the problem to provide an impartial evaluation.

Secondly, we can continue to study in a way which brings our level of knowledge into clearer focus, a process which I hope this book will contribute towards.

CONSCIOUS COMPETENCE

Noel Burch developed the conscious competence ladder in the 1970s while he was working for Gordon Training International, an organisation set up by the American clinical psychologist, Thomas Gordon. According to the model, there are four stages that we move through when learning a new skill:

1. **Unconsciously unskilled:** We are unaware that we don't possess this skill, or that we need to learn it.

Now, this can be a nice place to be. We have no idea that we don't have this skill, nor do we have any concept of needing it. We could call this a state of blissful ignorance. Mechanical skills in training are a good example of this. We may have trained, for many years, without really considering our own mechanical skills and the effect they have on the success of our dog.

2. **Consciously unskilled:** We know that we don't possess this skill.

This can be an uncomfortable place to be. It's where the door to new knowledge and skills has been opened, and we have to decide whether to step through it. For behaviourists, this can be the time when clients fail to follow a behavioural plan, or for those of us with fearful dogs, it can seem as if a chasm has opened up beneath us, as we start to understand the changes in routine we need to make.

This is where a skilled behaviourist will consider the pace with which they ask clients to work and take on new knowledge and skills. There is no more need to set unachievable criteria, and expectations, with clients than there is with their dogs.

3. **Consciously skilled:** We now know that we possess this skill and knowledge we need.

We put our learning into practice regularly and gain even more confidence as those new skills are applied. We may now, for example, have the skill to assess a situation, at speed, and decide if our fearful dog will be able to cope, or if we need to take avoiding action.

We still need to concentrate when we perform these activities, but, as we practise and gain more experience, they seem to become increasingly automatic.

4. **Unconsciously skilled:** We know that we possess this skill, but because we don't focus on it – as it is so easy – we seem to be unconsciously skilled at it.

This final stage is like driving a car when we have held a licence for many years. It is as if the car drives itself because we don't need to think: "now I need to change gear" or "now I should turn the steering wheel". However, it is also very important to remember how it felt when we were learning how to drive. How overwhelming it felt to steer, change gear and look in the mirror all at the same time.

When we are very familiar with a protocol for helping a fearful dog, we can forget how it felt to be back at stage two – when we were consciously unskilled. If we are to be successful, we need to acknowledge the challenges and consider how we can help ourselves, and our clients, to be skilled so that in turn, our dogs can acquire the skills they need.

RESISTANCE TO CHANGE

We know that we need to take action to help our fearful dog, we hire a behaviourist to help, and we are keen to implement the programme they have carefully devised. But, a few weeks later when they call to see how we are doing, we are embarrassed to admit that we have not made much progress.

From the behaviourist's perspective, that can be pretty confusing. The client has recognised that there is an issue that needs addressing. They have scheduled the appointment, paid for it, attended the consult and provided all the information for a behavioural plan to be devised. The behaviourist has listened to the client explain the impact that the fear has been having on both their dog and the family – and then, nothing.

It turns out that us humans are not so good at change. However, once we have an awareness of why this is the case, we can put together strategies to avoid those pitfalls.

BEING READY TO CHANGE

Considering change is a very different proposition to implementing change. There are no two ways about it, change can be difficult. Many of us already have full days and little free time, and now it's being suggested that we need to fit in even more tasks if we want to help our fearful dog.

This is the point at which the behaviourist, or the client, need to decide how important it is to help

the dog overcome his fears. Some situations may just need management. For example, a dog, who is scared of crowds, need never be placed in that situation. Or, perhaps, the problem only arises for a few weeks in a year when fireworks are going off.

More than likely, we all have a fear of something that has a very minor impact on our day-to-day lives, and so we have little motivation to change. The payoff for committing our time and energy to that type of fear is going to be minimal. If, however, that fear is having a considerable impact on our quality of life, we may consider that the time spent is well invested.

This is where we carry out a quick cost/benefit analysis before taking action. The cost may be in financial terms, so that might be the monetary cost of hiring a behaviourist, or it could be the amount of time we need to invest in the process. The benefit is the degree to which the situation is improved by committing to the cost.

To clarify, here is an example of the cost/benefit analysis in action. My dogs jump on me when I come home; it's a bit of an annoyance but, really, no big deal to me. Despite knowing how to fix this, I haven't invested the time in training an alternative greeting behaviour. The benefit of having dogs who don't jump up is not enough to justify the cost, in terms of my time.

Now I know that some of you, who are reading this confession, will be smiling and agreeing as you think of your own dogs. Others will find it frustrating and confusing as to why anyone would not simply train a polite greeting. So, this gives us another aspect to consider. Although we perceive something to be important, don't fall into the trap of assuming that others share the same viewpoint.

Therefore, before leaping in with a behaviour modification plan, we need to assess the readiness to change, and that is equally applicable if you are the owner, or the behaviourist.

SCALE OF READINESS

For us to go through the upheaval that change can bring, there needs to be a strong motivation for it to take place. I find it useful to ask a client: "On a scale of 1 to 10, how much does your dog's fear create problems for you?". This then provides me with an insight into how ready the client is to change, and how they interpret the severity of the situation.

Of course, everyone has a slightly different interpretation of what classifies as a 1 or a 10, but that, too, provides us with a deeper understanding of the situation. These types of questions allow us to dig deeper: "A 10? That sounds like a really tough situation, tell me about the problems it's causing". At this point, the client may reveal a situation that is

causing immense issues for the family and distressing fear for the dog. Or we might find that the client's perception of what constitutes a 10 is quite different from our own.

Now it is important to appreciate that the situation is still a 10 for the client, with all its entangled stress and worry, regardless of our opinion or how we assess the problem. If we just take down a case history, without checking the impact on the client, we may have failed to understand how distressing the situation is for them. However, if we acquire this insider information, we can effectively empathise, and reassure, the client.

Perhaps the client comes up with an assessment of a 3? Now we can ask: "A 3? That would seem to imply that the fear doesn't create too many problems. Tell me more about why it's important for you to get this issue resolved". The client may now explain that a friend or relative suggested they get help, or perhaps they are worried about the situation getting worse over time. Whatever the reason, we will, again, have a far greater understanding of their motivation for seeking help.

The other consideration, when the fear is assessed as a 'low problem' issue, is that it may reveal that the client is not aware of the gravity of the situation. Delving deeper, and asking further questions, may well unearth that the client's

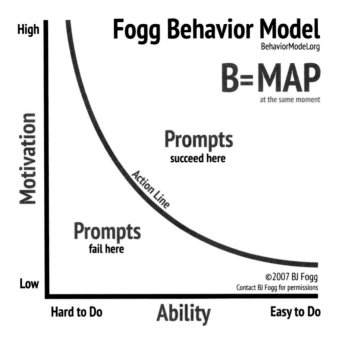

interpretation of their dog's responses may be flawed. For example, the dog who stands very still when another dog rushes over to "say hello", may not be indicative of the "calmness" the client is describing.

THE FOGG BEHAVIOUR MODEL

How would it be if we could predict the likelihood of success? If we could do this with some certainty, then we could address the limiting factors that may reduce the likely success of the behaviour modification plan. When you own a fearful dog, the last thing you need is more problems, or stress, from set-ups that are not going to achieve success. Equally, as a behaviourist, being able to assess how likely that your plan is going to be implemented, through to completion, will allow you to address any barriers early on in the process.

The Fogg Behaviour Model (FBM) is named after its designer, Dr BJ Fogg, who founded the Behavior Design Lab at Stanford University in the United States.

This model tells us that there are three elements that must come together at the same moment to achieve the behaviour we want:

behaviour = motivation x ability x trigger.

If one of these elements is missing, the behaviour is not going to take place. Therefore, using the FBM as a guide, we can quickly identify what stops ourselves, or our clients, from performing the behaviours that are needed.

When working with a client, there are, therefore, three questions we need to ask:

1. Is the client sufficiently motivated?
2. Does the client have the capabilities of performing the desired behaviour?
3. Did we remind the client to perform the desired behaviour?

Let us now look at each of these three questions in more detail.

MOTIVATION

Fogg suggests that there are three types of motivator, and each motivator embraces opposite ends of a spectrum:

1. **Sensation: pleasure-pain.** Unsurprisingly, we are more likely to perform a behaviour if it results in pleasure and less likely if it means experiencing pain. However, it is important to appreciate that we don't all experience pleasure and pain in the same way. To use a training analogy, we don't all value the same reinforcers, and what is punishing for one person may not be for another. If we are using an approach to work with a fearful dog, which is not pleasurable, we are probably not going to stick at it too long.

2. **Anticipation: hope-fear.** The second core motivator in this model is characterised by anticipation of an outcome. Hope is the anticipation of something good happening. Fear is the anticipation of something bad. This dimension can, at times, be more powerful than pleasure/pain. For example, in some situations, people will accept pain (purchasing car breakdown cover) in order to overcome fear (the worry of getting a puncture on the motorway).

If the prospect of implementing a particular behaviour modification plan is making a client feel anxious, they now have another hurdle to cross before they can get started. When a behaviourist is able to produce a plan, which fills the client with hope and positivity for helping their fearful dog, they are far more likely to get stuck in.

Hope is a very ethical and empowering motivator and something which we can assess on a regular basis. If we find our levels of hope are declining, that is a big red flag warning that we need to understand why that is happening. Is it that we don't feel that the approach is having any positive effect, or is that we don't feel we have the skills to implement the plan? Either way, spending some time reflecting on what has caused our feeling of hope to diminish will enable us to make changes or seek help.

3. **Belonging: social acceptance-social rejection:** As you probably know from your own life experiences, people are motivated to do things that win them social acceptance and status, even if these seem to be at odds with what is best for them in the long term. Equally, people tend to be especially motivated to avoid negative

consequences, such as being socially rejected.

So, how does that impact on our success in assisting a fearful dog? Well, everyone who comes into contact with the dog needs to be in agreement about how the situation is managed and progressed. If there is no agreement, it's going to create tension. One way of relieving that situation will be to relent and not push forward with the plan.

ABILITY

To perform the desired behaviour, a person must have the relevant ability. That seems really obvious, but if we are not careful, we can make assumptions.

Fogg suggests that there are two pathways to increasing ability. You could train people, over time, to give them the depth of skill and ability needed to undertake the complete target behaviour. Or, you could make the target behaviour easier to perform. By focusing on the simplicity of the behaviour, you increase ability. Doesn't that sound familiar to setting criteria for our fearful dogs to increase the likelihood of success? Well, it's just the same for us humans.

There are six simplicity factors:

1. **Time:** If a target behaviour requires time, and we don't have that time available, then the behaviour is not simple.

2. **Money:** If financial resources are limited, a behaviour that costs money is not simple. This then means that the link in the simplicity chain will break easily.

3. **Physical effort:** Behaviours that require physical effort may not be simple if there are mobility or physical limitations. What may seem like a straightforward request to walk, click and provide reinforcement, for example, could be completely unfeasible for someone who needs to focus all their attention on the process of walking.

4. **Brain cycles:** If performing a target behaviour requires intense concentration, it may not be simple. This is especially true if our minds are consumed with other issues, which could be a child having problems at school, a challenging boss or an upcoming house move.

5. **Social deviance:** This means going against the norm, and breaking what may be unwritten rules of society. If a target behaviour requires a degree of social deviance, then that behaviour is no longer straightforward. For example, the client is advised against reprimanding a dog when he growls at a passer-by. The client may know that telling off the dog is not going to be helpful, and may actually exacerbate the problem, but society believes that growls are 'bad

behaviour' and need punishing. This does not mean to say that the client condones reprimanding the dog. Instead, a strategy is required to cope with this situation.

6. **Non-routine:** People tend to find behaviours simple to complete if they are routine, so that means activities they do over and over again. We may think of these as being habits, or as operating on autopilot. When faced with a behaviour that isn't routine, a client may not find it simple. In seeking simplicity, people will often stick to their routine activities or habits.

TRIGGER

Now, this is an area that we dog people are very familiar with because we could swap the word 'trigger' for 'cue'. This means that we need to consider what the cues are for the new behaviour to happen. If we are unsure of the signs that indicate a dog is becoming overwhelmed, we are not going to be able to implement the strategy to help him.

This is where advance planning is needed to design clearly defined triggers for the new behaviour. For example, a management strategy for a dog fearful of strangers might be:
'when the doorbell rings, put Fido in the kitchen'. The doorbell is the cue, and the new behaviour is to put the dog in the kitchen.

One of the reasons that I use the Fogg Behaviour Model in canine behavioural consults is that the focus is on making things easier to get the right behaviour. If my clients find it easier to implement change, then it's more likely to happen.

BELIEF STRUCTURES

Beliefs are our brain's way of making sense of our complex world. They provide the details of the ways in which our brains expect things to happen, and how things should relate to each other. We could consider beliefs to be templates and that is because the brain is such an energy-expensive organ, it needs some shortcuts.

Beliefs allow the brain to predict what should happen in any situation, although this does mean some jumping to conclusions. For example, beliefs are often concerned with understanding the causes of things: If 'b' closely followed 'a', then 'a' might be assumed to have been the cause of 'b'.

These shortcuts to interpreting and predicting our world often involve connecting dots and filling in gaps. This can mean making assumptions based on incomplete information and based on similarity to previously recognised patterns. In jumping to conclusions, our brains have a preference for familiar conclusions over unfamiliar ones. So, that does mean that our brains are prone to error, sometimes seeing patterns where there are none. Sometimes errors might be identified and corrected; other times this will not be the case. It's a trade-off between efficiency and accuracy.

In its need for economy, and efficiency of energy consumption, the default tendency of the brain is to fit new information into its existing framework for understanding the world, rather than repeatedly reconstructing that framework from scratch. So, a dog who growls is a bad thing, right? That's certainly what many of us learnt as children. However, a fearful dog who has the confidence to growl, and communicate his discomfort, gives us an enormous advantage in understanding his emotional state. Of course, we want to avoid situations where growling is needed but, should it happen, we want the dog to be able to tell us so that we can take immediate action to change the environment. Without exception, I have explained this logic to every client I have helped with a fearful dog. On each occasion, their belief structure has informed them that growling is a bad thing which needs to be stopped – not that the environment needs to change which would then mean that growling was no longer necessary.

At this point, the client has a choice. They can either form a new belief to call on next time their dog is growling, or they can defend their current way of thinking. One reason why we resist changing our beliefs is because they are deeply entwined with how we define ourselves as people—our self-concept. If you consider yourself to be an experienced dog owner, and along comes a behaviourist who suggests that your interpretation of growling is incorrect, that self-concept is threatened.

So, the option is to accept the new way of thinking and develop a new belief structure, or to rationalise the existing belief and try to preserve a consistent self-image. It can be embarrassing to admit that we are fundamentally wrong.

In many cases, people have made a big personal investment in their belief system. They may have staked their reputation on a particular belief, such as having a specific way of training dogs or rehabilitating fearful ones. The investment in this belief may go far beyond a sense of self, extending to large material and financial investments, or a lifetime's career. For such a person, a change of belief would involve a monumental upheaval. No wonder it can be so hard to change our beliefs.

CAN WE CHANGE BELIEFS?

We can! I am sure you can think of beliefs you have held during your training career or as a dog owner? I remember the dominance rules being explained to me, such as 'you must eat before your dog '. I carefully followed each rule just in case my dogs became mutinous and took over the household! Today my dogs eat first, and there are still no signs of a rebellion. Luckily, for me, this was very early in my career, and so I had little to lose in terms of reputation or earnings when I quickly realised that the rules didn't make an awful lot of sense.

When we are working with clients who have fearful dogs, there can be all kinds of beliefs that may interfere with how we perceive the case needs to be handled. Of course, we could just tell the client that they are wrong and that they need to change their opinion. But that runs the risk of losing the client and not being able to assist a dog who desperately needs our help.

The canine behaviourist experiences an extra layer of concern in these situations. They are all too aware that, should, in this example, a fearful dog be reprimanded for growling, then he may escalate his warning communication to the next stage – a snap. If that is punished then the dog may be left with few options other than to bite. Then the outcome for the dog, who was simply communicating in one of the only ways left to him, is not looking good. So that can mean that the behaviourist can feel immense pressure to change the client's opinion.

You could assume that once someone is faced with the 'facts', they have little choice but to change their minds.

However, beliefs are not just cold, mental templates; they are intertwined with our emotions. So, it should be no surprise that when we feel that our beliefs have been challenged, we might feel threatened and then react defensively.

There are many psychological models which describe how we can most effectively change a long-held belief. From these I have pulled out five key considerations:

We are heavily influenced by who communicates the information: The feelings we have about the messenger can cause us to be irrational and discard advice given by someone we dislike. So, while we are not aiming for the client to become a life-long friend, we do need to understand the positive influence that effective communication skills can have.

Norms: We tend to do what those around us are already doing. Telling people what others do in a similar situation can be very powerful.

Self-affirmation: When we are faced with information that threatens our self-esteem, we often respond defensively. The psychology of self-affirmation suggests that, even simple reminders of self-worth, may be enough to reduce this knee-jerk response. This means that when we look for opportunities to gain agreement, along with recognising the client's strengths, they may be more likely to consider our perspective. The overkill backfire effect: Ensure that your explanation is brief and straightforward. Use clear language and images where appropriate. You may be able to cite the research that substantiates your perspective, but if the misinformation is simpler and more compelling than yours, then it's also going to be more attractive.

Focus on the benefits. When you present new information, focus on the potential benefits it can bring rather than dwelling on the threats of the old belief. There is no need to 'rub salt in the wound' by focusing on how we perceive the client to be 'wrong'.

SUMMARY

For the Behaviourist: We cannot underestimate the impact that understanding, and applying theories of human psychology, will have on whether we are able to help a client's fearful dog. Many of us are drawn to becoming behaviourists because of a love of dogs and a passion for helping them live better lives. However, it's essential that we also understand the factors which can lead us to success in our relationship with the human end of the lead.

For the owner of a fearful dog:
Reflecting on how we think, act, and respond is an essential part of helping fearful dogs to learn new ways of dealing with difficult situations. Our dogs are learning all the time, even when we are not intentionally engaged in a teaching process. As a result, every interaction we have with them either reconfirms their understanding of us, or teaches them something new about the relationship we have. Being aware of our biases and our preconceptions can help us to challenge unhelpful beliefs and to discover new ways of helping our fearful dogs.

This chapter provides advice for owners on how to plan for the arrival of a dog with known fearful responses, or for those dogs who may initially be overwhelmed when in a home environment. For behaviourists and trainers, the ideas and suggestions that follow will provide a good foundation on which you can then commence your behaviour plan.

When a fearful dog, is up for rehoming, it's likely that they have either missed out on the opportunity for effective socialisation and habituation when young, or that life experiences have caused them to react in a fearful way. Realistic expectations will ensure that the new owner is equipped with knowledge of some of the challenges they may encounter as their new companion learns how to trust and relax in his home.

The new owner might be in the position of having full details of their dog's fear and will, therefore, know when it is likely to occur. This might happen when adopting from a rescue organisation and the staff have seen the response within the kennel environment. Alternatively, a behavioural assessment carried out by the rescue may have indicated towards potential problems.

However, it can be very difficult to make an accurate assessment when a dog is in rescue. Kennels are generally noisy places with lots of activity throughout the day. For dogs who have never been in that environment before, it can be completely overwhelming. So we sometimes see dogs, who display immense fear when they are in rescue, but never show it again once they can relax and chill out in their new home.

Then there are the dogs who are very confident in the kennel environment. Some of the hunting dogs in Spain, and puppy farm dogs across the world, have only ever known that situation; they have never crossed the threshold into a home. For these dogs, the change in environment from kennel to the house is immense, and they then begin to show fears, which have not been seen previously.

This is why it is so important that the new owner is completely honest with both the rescue organisation, and with themselves, when considering the type of dog they can rehome. Seeing a terrified dog blossom into a confident companion is, without a doubt, incredibly rewarding. However, taking on a fearful dog can mean significant changes to your routine and social life, with the prospect of some heartache, self-doubt, and a number of tough days along the way.

PLANNING

In most situations, the new owner will have a degree of control over when their adoptee comes home. This provides the opportunity to gather together everything that will be needed and to organise the home environment before the dog arrives.

CRATE TRAINING

While the subject of crates can provoke a whole range of opinions, when a dog has travelled a distance, or is coming from abroad, a good rescue organisation will have carried out some crate training in advance. This means that a crate in the home will have some familiarity and a history of reinforcement. It provides safe retreat for the dog and peace of mind for the new owner.

HARNESS, COLLAR AND LEAD

I strongly recommend the Haqihana double h harness, combined with a collar and a double-ended lead. This style of harness has an extra strap going under the dog's chest, making it virtually impossible for him to back out of it. When combined with a well-fitting collar and a lead, which attaches to both, the new owner should have complete confidence when transporting and walking their new arrival.

GIVING TIME

Too often, I am called to cases where a rescue dog has been collected on a Saturday morning, had lots of time with the family over the weekend, and then everyone returns to work/school on a Monday morning. Not too surprisingly, they return to a scene of devastation on Monday evening. A dog who has grown up in a home, and has no fears, may cope with this situation very well. However, a fearful dog, or one who is coming into the house for the first time, is going to struggle with this dramatic change in environment and then the sudden disappearance of their new family after the weekend is finished. The new owner should aim to spend at least two weeks with their fearful dog before leaving him for any length of time.

SCHEDULING TIME APART

Now I know that I have just recommended that the new owner needs to put aside two weeks to spend with a new arrival, but it is equally important to schedule some time apart, within the home, right from day one. The temptation will be to spend as much time as possible with the dog, and show him that people need not be a source of fear. However, there are several risks to this approach. You may quickly develop that trust but, in doing so, there is the potential for developing hyper-attachment. Hyper-attachment refers to a situation when the dog becomes anxious when a specific attachment figure is absent, and who gains little comfort by the presence of other people. Typically the dog wants to always be by your side and follows you from room to room.

There is some debate as to whether hyper-attachment is associated with separation anxiety. Some research indicates there is no connection, while another school of thought believes there is an association between the two. Either way, we should consider whether a dog's inability to settle, without continually following a person around, is really indicative of a balanced emotional response.

Students and clients will be familiar with my mantra of always planning to avoid additional work. By scheduling time apart from day one, the new owner is developing a dog who sees this as normal and who is building an emotional resilience to spending time apart. The aim is to set the dog up for success by proceeding gradually, ensuring he acquires the requisite behaviours before raising the criteria to another achievable level. This means very short periods of absence, which gives him the chance to learn how to relax both with and without his new owner.

For the dog with fear of people, an additional reason for not being a constant presence in their environment, is the risk of flooding. Flooding is fully discussed in Chapter 12: Don't Go There Techniques but, briefly, it creates a situation from which the dog cannot escape while the source of his fear is present. The theory is that the dog will discover that the fear is unsubstantiated and will learn a new response to the situation. However, there are many risks with this strategy, and by not allowing a fearful dog to have time away from his new owner, they become a very real possibility.

Achieving some physical distance from dog and owner may be as simple as having a stair-gate between one room and another. The owner can sit and read a book or catch up on emails, while the dog is enjoying a tasty chew on his bed from the other side of the gate.

KEEPING VISITORS AWAY

The new owner may well be besieged with requests from friends and family who are keen to meet the new arrival. They will come with the very best of intentions but, for the fearful dog, this onslaught of new people may be too much to cope with.

Setting criteria can be a great way of deciding when the time is right for your dog to be introduced to new people. It might be that you need your dog to be relaxed when you enter the room and for him to be confident enough to come to you for attention. If your dog is still fearful of you, it is certainly not the time for him to meet anyone else.

To build up trust in people when it has

been eroded, takes time and – during that time – there needs to be some predictability of interactions. With the best will in the world, it's difficult to control the behaviour of other people, so new owners should not feel pressurised into creating more work for themselves by even trying!

ENRICHMENT

Environmental enrichment provides opportunities for your dog to be stimulated and challenged in a way that promotes their normal range of behaviours, while not getting into trouble. So, chewing is a normal canine behaviour, but it requires the owner to provide appropriate items to chew on, rather than allowing the dog to find his own, probably inappropriate item.

Nose work provides the opportunity for enrichment, which doesn't need direction from a person, so this then makes it perfect for the dog who may be fearful of human contact. It is thought that foraging behaviour turns on what neuroscientist, Jaak Panksepp, calls the 'seeking circuit' or 'seeker system'. This system makes animals intensely interested in exploring their world, becoming excited when they discover their 'find'.

This part of the brain is also responsible for the release of dopamine, the neurotransmitter that is connected to feelings of motivation and reward. By allowing a dog to sniff, you are allowing

him to experience the feel-good factor of dopamine, which can, in turn, lower anxiety. Researchers, Duranton and Horowitz (2018: *Let me sniff! Nosework induces positive judgment bias in pet dogs', Applied Animal Behaviour Science*) have concluded that when a dog uses his nose to find hidden food, it can even increase his sense of optimism. Scent game enrichment can be as simple as tossing treats on the floor for the dog to find through to elaborate set-ups for him to search and find a hidden scent.

For some fearful dogs, eating is incompatible with the presence of people, so you may need to use a secluded space – such as the garden – for a food scatter and then allow your dog to sniff out the treats. The first few nose games should be very easy so that he understands the game but, remember, a dog's sense of smell is far superior to our own so he can then be given space, and time, to work through the search by himself.

Fearful dogs can also be reluctant to interact with new items, such as food enrichment toys. For a fearful dog, the focus is on staying alive and avoiding anything that is going to cause him harm, so it's no wonder that he avoids something new, which may be another threat. That said, part of reducing fear also relates to new experiences and building confidence. The key, here, is in ensuring that the experience is planned to cause little anxiety and is sufficiently reinforcing to encourage more exploratory behaviour.

To give an example, a dog may avoid a stuffed Kong – even though it may smell temptingly of food – if its appearance is new. Nature is full of instances where the bold individuals of a species may be the ones to have their pick of the harvest, but they are also the first to be devoured by the predator! So the new owner should introduce the food-stuffed toy by holding it in their hand, pulling out the treats, and then offering them to their dog. A few days of repetition is generally enough for the dog to decide that the Kong is no longer a threat, and he will have the confidence to approach it on his own.

WALKS

It takes time to build trust and to identify the situations that cause a fearful response. With this in mind, I strongly recommend that the new owner does not go out for walks during the first week of their dog's arrival. This provides him with the opportunity to decompress from the inevitable stress of travel, and his new home surroundings, without having to cope with the additional smells, sounds and sights which he will encounter on a walk. Instead, the new owner should take the time to find out more about their dog: where that spot is that he loves being stroked, which treat is his favourite and what toys he likes to play with. During the first week,

the owner may also identify particular scenarios, raised voices or children running, for example, which could trigger a fearful response. It is far better to identify these in the safety of the home rather than when out on a walk.

When the time comes to go out for a walk, I strongly advise new owners to stick to the same route for two weeks. Generally, I also ask them to plan that route so that it doesn't involve driving to a destination. During these walks, the dog will learn the route, and he will know how to get home, should the worst-case scenario happen and he gets loose. The exception is if the owner is lucky enough to have access to a fully enclosed exercise area that can be hired for their exclusive use. Even so, the perimeters must be checked for safety before allowing the dog to run free and explore; a fearful dog can show incredible agility in a flight response from a perceived danger. Remember to attach a light long line to the harness so that you can connect more easily when it's time to go home.

Remember, this is the dog's time to explore rather than it being the owner's exercise for the day. This change of emphasis means that if the fearful dog wants to sniff a particularly smelly spot for a few minutes, it is absolutely okay. It is also okay to stop and take in the world for a moment, which is not a bad philosophy for dog and human alike!

This chapter considers the planning needed to successfully work with fearful dogs.

Whatever technique you utilise, be it desensitisation, the targeted approach protocol or one of the others described in this book, the planning and assessment which takes place before the implementation can be instrumental in deciding whether your approach will be successful.

The treatment of fear does not necessarily require the knowledge of how, or why, the issue arose. At times not knowing can actually be beneficial in ensuring that you are not misled by well-intentioned, but inaccurate, information. That said, whether you are the owner of the fearful dog, or a behaviourist assisting a client, there are still a number of questions to ask and information to gather. This will be instrumental in helping you to decide on the best plan of action.

If you are working with a client, I strongly recommend that you review Chapter Three: The Human Factor in Canine Fear before the behavioural consult. Understanding the client's motivations, and being able to assess their willingness to change, will allow you to work out how you can most effectively provide assistance.

If you are working with your own fearful dog, this chapter may seem very orientated towards the behaviourist and client. However, it can be challenging to make an accurate assessment of what is happening with our own dogs. Our relationship, preconceptions and beliefs can interfere with accurate observation. With this in mind, it can be useful to approach the situation with your own dog as if it you were working with a client; keep the diary, delve into the triggers, and so on, to develop a clear picture of what is happening.

UNDERSTANDING THE ISSUES

I suspect that I am not the only behaviourist who has been called out to see an "aggressive" dog who was attacking another dog in the family. However I clearly remember one case where I found the "aggressor" providing a lovely demonstration of a play bow and an invite to a game. The accompanying 'growling' caused the owner to become concerned, and she had sensibly got a second opinion to find out what was happening.

Research carried out in 2012 by Michele Wan, and her team of researchers, at Columbia University in New York, set out to see how well four different groups of people were able to assess happiness and fear in dogs. These were:

1. Non-owners.
2. Owners.
3. Dog professionals with less than 10 years of experience.
4. Dog professionals with more than 10 years of experience.

A panel of canine behaviour experts had assessed the videos, prior to the start of the research, with each one being categorised as demonstrating either happiness or fear. The participants were asked to consider four factors for each video:

1. Decide on the emotion being displayed by the dog from a choice of angry, fearful, happy, sad or neutral.
2. Describe the specific features of the dog that led them to their conclusion. So, this might be the position of the dog's tail or whether the dog's ears were flat to their head.
3. Rate the difficulty that they experienced in interpreting each dog's emotions.
4. Rate how accurate they believed they were in their assessment of the dogs.

Interestingly most people – over 90 per cent, who took part – were able to correctly identify the happy dogs. However, when it came to recognising fear in dogs, 70 per cent of dog professionals, 60 per cent of dog owners, and only 35 per cent of non-owners were able to assess the dogs in the video correctly. The features that participants used to make their decisions also varied with their level of experience. Those with more experience tended to focus on a dog's facial features. Inexperienced participants tended to be led by the dog's tail and body posture.

So, what does this all mean? Well, the potential for misunderstanding a dog's communication, as we have seen, can be immense. Even if you are working with your own dog, I strongly recommend writing down a list of the body language you see when your dog is fearful. While this may confirm your thinking on what is happening, it also provides you with a checklist to refer to as you work through a fear reducing protocol.

Some clients offer to video the dog to provide 'evidence' of the fear. While this can be an option where the fear is unavoidable, such as an essential visit to the vet, I generally ask clients not to set-up situations to cause the fear to take place. I don't want to be in a position where it leads to an escalation of the problem.

If you don't have the knowledge, it can be challenging to explain what is happening and, as mentioned earlier, poor-quality information can result in unhelpful behavioural plans. There has been a wide range of questionnaires developed to measure fearfulness in dogs. However, all of them require some background knowledge in order to understand what may be happening. For example, an evaluation will be needed to back up a statement such as "my dog gets nervous easily". It is highly likely that my evaluation of "nervous" is different to yours, as is the concept of it happening "easily".

A further example from a questionnaire is the statement, "my dog becomes very shy when unknown visitors come to the home". Now this may have more detail, but it still provides little information to enable a clear understanding of what is taking place.

To gain accurate information, I take a two-pronged approach. Firstly, I ask clients to keep a diary leading up to the consult, which is usually scheduled a few weeks from the first point of contact. In the diary, the client makes notes of when the dog showed fear, the circumstances around it, and then describes how the dog responded. This allows for an almost immediate recording of information before the accuracy, and recall, of the situation, begin to dissipate. Information on who was involved, when it happened, and what happened, should also be noted.

I also provide clients with the URLs for several online video clips that show fearful and aggressive dogs. I then ask them to consider how the dogs in the videos compare to their own dog's reaction. In doing this the client doesn't need to know how to accurately describe the carriage of their dog's tail, or the position of his ears, they simply need to match what is happening to what they see on their screen. Interestingly, I often get very detailed information from this, with clients telling me for example that their dog's tail is the same as the dog in video one, but then their ears are like the one in video four. The additional benefit of this is that all the information – the diary and video clips – are provided in advance of the consult.

So, at this point, we have a good idea of how the dog responds. Now we need to dig deeper to understand the triggers that are causing the fear.

IDENTIFYING TRIGGERS

Detailed information allows you to devise a very targeted behaviour plan. If, for example, the fear is stated to be "of people" then we have to assume that we may need to go through a comprehensive process of generalisation. This means that the dog is able to transfer his understanding from one situation to next. So, a dog who has learnt that female adults are no longer to be feared, may need to repeat the learning process with male adults and children to come to the same conclusion.

In some situations, generalisation may need to be extensive so that the dog becomes less fearful about particular characteristics of, for example, male adults. This might include:

- with walking sticks
- running
- wearing hats
- with a beard
- different heights
- different builds
- characteristics such as being louder, more – exuberant, more expressive body language

If, however, coming back to our example of a dog who is fearful of people, it can be narrowed down to be "of children", we now have a more specific point of reference.

From here, we can consider whether it's all children or whether it's those who are around five years old or younger.

Considering those under-fives: what if they are sitting quietly? Is that still a problem or is it only when they are running around?

If they running around outside when the dog is in the house, is that okay?

So you can see we have gone from "fear of people" through to "fear of under-fives when they are running around in the same area as the dog". As you can imagine, the behavioural plan is going to be quite different now you have a specific trigger to work with.

MANAGEMENT

As the behaviour modification plan is put into action, there will be a period during which we will want to avoid the dog's exposure to the fear-inducing stimulus. For example, can the dog be in another part of the home while the young children are running around? I have a strong belief that, in most pet situations, the longer the reliance on management, the higher the risk that it will break down at some point. We don't expect our dogs to be 100 per cent reliable in their responses, and it's unrealistic to think that we would be either. It just takes a moment of distraction to forget to close a door, and the fearful dog is in the midst of a trigger-inducing scenario.

When the outcome of a management breakdown has a significant repercussion, look for set-ups which give leeway to a mistake happening.

These are the types of situations where a dog may respond aggressively or where their fear is such that, if he were to get out of the home, there would be difficulty in getting him back again. Leeway might be achieved as simply as setting up puppy playpen panels in front of a critical doorway. This requires you to close a door and then pull across the panels, so even If the door didn't shut properly, you have the panels across the doorway to prevent an exit. Using a harness and a collar, along with a double-ended lead, is another way of providing that leeway; if the dog slips the collar or backs out of a harness, you still have a back up.

Accepting that mistakes will happen, but planning to minimise their likelihood, reduces some of the pressure on care providers of the fearful dog.

MAINTAINING ROUTINE DURING BEHAVIOURAL INTERVENTIONS

While working with a dog to help him overcome his fears, I suggest that you take a good look at his day-to-day routine. The aim is to identify how we can include, and maintain, predictability while reducing the sources of stress.

Predictability might mean that, after a morning walk, the dog has his breakfast and then a quiet time until midday. Everyone in the home knows that during the dog's quiet time, they are not to approach or seek interaction with him. Again, we need to make this type of management easy for everyone to get right. So, if the dog is happy in his crate, allow him relax in there. Alternatively he could be in a room, which has little human traffic, with a stair gate across the doorway.

In some situations, such as where there are lots of people in a busy home, I add a visual signal to remind everyone it's quiet time for their dog. A red bandana tied to the crate front, or on to the stair-gate, is a great way to remind everyone that they should leave the dog alone, and it is one that children quickly understand and follow. Do be prepared for the child to ask for their own red bandana to signal they also want quiet time; it happens a lot!

IDENTIFICATION AND REDUCTION OF STRESSORS

Reducing the overall stress for the fearful dog means that he can switch from being in a fight/flight state to one in which he can learn new responses to the feared stimuli.

Identifying, and then minimising the impact, of sources of stress may mean restricting the fearful dog's interactions with people he finds challenging. This might be very young children, who may not be gentle in their touch, or people who tend to be loud and very demonstrative in their body language. It might also relate to interactions with other dogs, whether it's a youngster who has yet to pick up on the signs to back off, or a fence-chasing dog when out on a walk.

Where there is generalised fear, which makes it challenging to reduce the stress level, medication may be an option to provide a window of opportunity for the behaviour modification plan to be successful. See *Chapter Ten: Psychopharmacological Options for more information on how medication can help in this situation*.

References

Wan M., Bolger, N. and Champagne, F.A. (2012). *'Human perception of fear in dogs varies according to experience with dogs.'* PLoS ONE, 7(12)

Going forward

In the following chapters I describe, in detail, the many different approaches we can take to help a dog become less fearful. Sadly, there is no single magic cure which will be the correct approach; this is very much about assessing the individual dog, their fears and their home environment. It may also be necessary to combine methods, such as the psychopharmacological options along with the behavioural approach of desensitisation.

I always advise clients that we may need to adjust the approach we take as we learn more about how the dog responds to the behaviour modification plan. This ensures that the client is aware that this may be necessary, and it helps to reconfirm that we should see their dog as having their own individual needs which may not be met with a generic approach.

This chapter includes background information on the technique of systematic desensitisation, a case study to demonstrate how the protocol can be applied, and a discussion of its limitations.

BACKGROUND

The process of systematic desensitisation was developed by South African psychologist, Joseph Wolpe, in the 1950s. Working with the cats of Wits University, Wolpe discovered that they could overcome their fears through gradual and systematic desensitisation. The approach is frequently used within the work of human behaviour modification for the treatment of phobias or fear. It is based on the theory that if mild versions are presented repeatedly, their lack of effect will generalise to more severe versions. Over time, it should be possible to introduce more severe stimuli until finally reaching the severity that caused the fearful response – but with the individual now remaining calm and relaxed. This is considered to be an example of reciprocal inhibition; our dogs cannot feel fear and relaxation at the same time.

The process of systematic desensitisation does not involve leaping straight in by introducing the very thing that causes the fearful response. When used with humans, there are three techniques to learn first which can help to encourage a calm state of mind:

Deep breathing: When we are anxious, we tend to do what is called chest breathing – taking rapid, shallow breaths. The problem with this is that it can disturb the oxygen and carbon dioxide levels in the body resulting in increased heart rate, dizziness and muscle tension – none of the things you would associate with feeling calm.

Progressive muscle relaxation: Through tensing or tightening one muscle group at a time, followed with the release of the tension, we can learn the difference between how it feels to have a tensed muscle compared to a completely relaxed muscle. With this knowledge, we can cue the relaxed state when we start to feel our muscles tensing as a result of fear or anxiety.

Visualisation: Imagining an idyllic, stress-free setting, such as sitting on a beautiful sandy beach, with a blue sky overhead and the sound of tropical birds in the background, may help us to reach a state of mental and physical relaxation.

Now you may be thinking that's all well

and good, but how do I teach my dog to visualise their stress-free setting? Well, that's one aspect of systematic desensitisation that we may not be able to transfer to helping our dogs overcome their fears. However, we can work on the parts that encourage a physically relaxed body, which, in turn, is likely to result in a relaxed and calm state of mind. The relaxed body language can then be placed on cue and utilised to help our dogs remain fear free in new or mildly fear inducing situations. We can then design a fear hierarchy to work out the least feared in each scenario for the dog, factoring in each step that needs to be taken before reaching the most feared situation. We are then, finally, ready to begin the desensitisation process.

IN PRACTICE

To see systematic desensitisation in practice, we are going to consider the case of Jack, a three-year-old Border Collie. Jack becomes very fearful when an unknown person comes through the gate into the garden that then leads towards the house. This response is specific to this environment; he can pass strangers in the street without becoming fearful.

THE FEAR HIERARCHY

When designing the fear hierarchy, we first need to consider what the dog can cope with, right now, without demonstrating any signs of fear. We can then work out the ultimate aim for the desensitisation programme.

In Jack's case, right now he demonstrates no fear when a stranger walks past the gate. The ultimate aim is for him to remain relaxed when a stranger enters the house and sits in a chair. We therefore need to consider each of the steps to get from where he is right now to achieving that ultimate aim.

Sitting in a chair

Entering the house

Stand at the door to the house

Walking down the garden path

Coming through the garden gate

Standing at the garden gate

Walking past the garden gate

The number of steps required is going to depend on the severity of the fearful response. An outline plan (see page 56) starts with a stranger walking past the garden gate – which does not provoke a fearful response – and works through stages to what would have caused the most fearful response – a stranger being in the house and sitting in a chair.

Do remember that a plan is just that. Sometimes we can create a detailed plan and find that we can skip a few stages as the dog responds much more quickly than we expected. In other cases, we might need to break a stage down into multiple components.

For example, in Jack's case, the stranger walking down the garden path may require several intermediate stages so that it becomes: the stranger taking one step inside the gate, then two steps, three steps etc. Careful and considered study of the dog's emotional state, and body language (see above) throughout the process will quickly tell you how to progress or when you need to reduce the criteria.

Becoming relaxed

Before we begin on the first steps of the fear hierarchy, we are going to teach Jack how to offer calm, relaxed behaviour. We will start teaching this in a quiet, non-distracting environment and then progress to more challenging situations through the process of generalisation. It's important that we,

SIGNS OF A FEARFUL DOG

For a quick reminder on body language, a fearful dog may display some or all of the following signs:

- Crouched body
- Pinned back ears
- Tail between the legs or tail held stiff
- 'Whale eye' where you can see more white of the eye than normal
- Tight mouth
- Frozen body position

again, focus on Jack's emotional state throughout this process. We also need to remind ourselves that this is not just a down stay that is being taught.

This part of the training forms the foundations for the desensitisation process. If the foundations are not as strong as they need to be, they will 'collapse' under the desensitisation process. This will then mean that instead of seeing a relaxed response from Jack as we introduce the things which cause fear, we are likely to see the fear re-emerging.

Criteria

Jack already knows the down position so we are going to use capturing to mark the calm behaviour (see page 51). However, 'mark calm behaviours' is very vague. So, before we begin the training, we need to be more specific about what we are looking for in order to mark it in a consistent way.

When Jack is relaxed at home, he lies down, leaning on one hip. We can then consider other, subtler, aspects of Jack's behaviour when he is relaxed. Soft eyes, calm breathing, tail position, relaxed mouth – these are all elements which are likely to be present. The ability to see, and identify, signs that a dog is relaxed will help us to mark the behaviour we want.

Once we have the relaxed behaviour in place, we will need to help Jack learn how to maintain the position through the addition of duration, and to perform the behaviour in a variety of situations. This will eventually allow him to maintain the behaviour in situations that currently cause him to be fearful. This process of generalisation is gradually developed, working at the easiest level through to the most challenging.

Capturing behaviours

Because these are behaviours which we know Jack frequently performs, and we can predict when they will be performed, capturing is a great technique to use. This, very simply, means that when Jack performs a behaviour we are looking for – such as lying on his side – we 'capture' it by marking and then reinforcing. Marking the behaviour is the means of communicating to the dog that the behaviour he just performed

was the right one, and reinforcement is on its way. This, in turn, increases the likelihood of that behaviour happening again.

Using a clicker to mark the behaviour may be the obvious choice here, but I would suggest checking the dog's emotional response to hearing the click first. If the dog becomes very excited at the sound, perhaps from previous training, then this is going to create the very opposite of the calm, relaxed behaviour we are looking for. So instead of a clicker, a calm and quiet marker word may help the dog to maintain, and develop, that relaxed state that we are aiming for.

Luring, through the use of food or toys to encourage the dog into the required position, is not part of the capturing technique, nor is physical manipulation. The benefit of the capturing technique is that, from the very start, the behaviour is offered without handler involvement. Therefore there is no lure, or hands-on physicality, to fade out.

Adding the cue

Once captured, we need to add a cue to the relaxation behaviour so that we can ask for the response once we move to the desensitisation phase of the programme. There can be a temptation to add the cue early in the process, but we want to ensure that Jack is readily offering the relaxed behaviour before we consider its addition.

We can do this by assessing how quickly the desired behaviour is offered. So, imagine that Jack has just performed the behaviour that we are looking for – laying on his hip, for example. We mark it and reinforce, which causes Jack to move position to eat the treat. What happens next? Does Jack immediately return to lay on his hip, awaiting the marker word, and more reinforcement? If so, then that is a good time to add the cue. Jack has clearly demonstrated that he understands what he has to do in order to receive the food. If there is a delay before the behaviour is repeated, then we need to establish greater understanding before the cue is added.

If we were to add the cue – and there was no response – the cue becomes meaningless. There is also the risk that we repeat the cue several times hoping that, with each repetition, the behaviour will be offered. This can either cement the dog's perception that the cue has no meaning, or that the cue is repeated several times before the behaviour is required. If we find ourselves giving the cue with fingers crossed, hoping we might get the right response, then this is not the right time to add it.

Once the cue has been added, we should be aiming towards minimal latency; that is, the time between giving the cue to the time that the dog commences the behaviour.

The length of time it takes to get into the desired down position will vary depending on the breed of dog. Imagine the difference between a young, agile Border Collie and a very large breed, such as a Newfoundland. However both dogs can commence the behaviour as soon as they hear the cue and so have zero latency.

Latency can be a good indication of the dog's understanding of the behaviour but also the desire to receive the reinforcement. Think how quickly you might start a behaviour if the reinforcement is something that you really want!

Training schedule

When we set out to capture behaviour, we want to set ourselves up for success. We, therefore, need to consider when the dog is most likely to offer that behaviour. In the case of Jack, once he has had his evening walk, he returns home and settles down for the evening. This, then, becomes the most opportune time of day to train.

Imagine, for a moment, trying to capture a calm, relaxed behaviour when a dog is full of energy and ready to go for a walk. He could still learn the behaviour, but it's going to be much more difficult for him. So we need to make it easier for everyone and find a time of day that matches the type of behaviour we are aiming to teach. Eventually we want to be able ask our dog to be calm, even in the context that had previously caused a fearful response but, right now, at this early stage, we want to set up everything to provide us with the greatest possible chance of success.

Reinforcement type and delivery

There are times when we can use a particular type of reinforcement, and its method of delivery, to generate excitement and energy. Imagine throwing a ball after a dog has performed a great recall. For many dogs, that is going to create speed and excitement. However, these are two things which we don't want Jack to demonstrate; we need steady and calm.

In this situation, a medium value food treat, which is calmly delivered, is much more likely to achieve success in the initial stages. For Jack, treats such as hot dogs and ham are much too exciting; when they are on offer he can struggle to focus. Cooked chicken, however, is still good but doesn't cause excitement and he can still focus and continue to follow cues.

So chicken is going to be the main reinforcement of choice for Jack. Now we need to consider how to deliver the reinforcement. As a herding breed, movement can cause Jack to become very excited and that is exactly what happens when food is thrown. It's a fun and exciting game, but that is not what we are looking for in the early stages of this training. So for Jack, we are going to deliver the chicken, by hand, directly to him.

There are times when a dog may not be hugely excited by food and so adding movement to its delivery can really increase its value. Be aware that adding in the movement will mean that the dog will leap out of his calm position to chase it. However, this is okay as it presents another opportunity for the dog to take up the relaxed position and be reinforced again. While this may take a little longer than if the dog were to stay in a relaxed position to receive the reinforcement, it's going to be quicker than using something which the dog doesn't find particularly reinforcing.

Also consider that the choice of reinforcement is unlikely to stay static. This is another situation where you need to observe the dog's responses to work out what is the right choice on that particular day, or in that particular environment.

There may be temptation to deliver a whole handful of chicken for a really good response, or a breakthrough in training, and this is often described as giving the dog a 'jackpot'. It's completely understandable that we want to celebrate when a dog suddenly offers the behaviour we are looking for. However, the problem is that jackpots can interfere with the rhythm of training, which may actually make it harder for the dog to learn. This is because, for learning to take place, we need to achieve several repetitions of the behaviour, ideally in quick succession.

So, for example, if you were teaching a dog to sit, you would work on a number of repetitions – sit/treat, sit/treat, sit/treat – and through these repetitions the dog would make a connection between sitting and getting a treat. This is just like us when we are learning something new; we need to repeat it several times so that we master what is required.

In contrast, if you go for a: sit/jackpot, you may find that by the time the dog has finished eating all the treats, he has forgotten what he did to cause the feeding frenzy! He will achieve far greater understanding if he is allowed the opportunity to practise the new skill a few times, and to make the connection between offering the behaviour and receiving a treat.

Using jackpots in training may be less of an issue for a dog who is experienced in the learning process but, why not simply make it easier?

So, when you get a breakthrough, a better plan is to reinforce as normal and then set up for another repetition. In this way you can double check that it was learning that was taking place, and not a fluke offering of the behaviour. When you get the behaviour three of four times in a row – end the session and then have a celebratory game with your dog!

Schedule of Reinforcement

There is a whole myriad of reinforcement schedules available to you, but I strongly suggest keeping things simple and utilising a continuous schedule of reinforcement. This means that reinforcement will be delivered every single time that the target behaviour meets the criteria that you have set. Variable schedules, where reinforcement is not given every time the criteria is met, can be useful when you may be asking for the behaviour in a situation where you cannot reinforce – but that is not going to be the case for Jack. A continuous schedule means that we will be able to build a huge history of reinforcement for calm behaviour, and that will help to establish it as the new response to the fear inducing situation.

Remember that we will be developing the criteria towards the end goal so we need to consider when to push the behaviour on to the next stage in the plan. A good measure may be a success rate of at least 80 per cent so, four times out of five, Jack lies down and then rolls over on to his right hip. This would demonstrate that he has developed an understanding of the required behaviour and that we can now move on to the next stage in the training plan.

The training process

Now the planning is complete, we can begin training. When Jack returns home after his evening walk, we can fetch the pot of chicken treats and then sit quietly and wait for first signs of that relaxed body language. We want to avoid a staring match – that is not, generally, the best way to get relaxation! So it might be better to be sitting at a table reading a book, but keeping an eye on the dog at the same time. The moment we see Jack shift his weight on to one hip we can capture that behaviour through marking and then reinforcing. Then we wait for the behaviour to be offered again.

Frequently, dogs associate a behaviour with the specific environment where it was learnt. For example, a dog may perform beautiful heelwork in the training class but then pull like crazy when on his daily walk. We want to ensure that Jack can perform his relaxed behaviour in a variety of locations, so we need to include generalisation within the training. This process simply means that our dogs learn to perform the behaviour no matter where they are, or what is happening around them

There are no fixed rules about when to commence generalisation, and so I recommend that you consider the individual dog. For example, is he the type who will be quick to ritualise behaviour, with strong beliefs in what he does in a particular situation? If so, he is likely to benefit from generalisations being added early in the process. If the dog is more flexible in his approach to what happens, then you might generalise behaviours when they are more developed.

Generalisation is not just about where the behaviour is performed, it can also include:

- Time of day – morning, daytime, evening, before and after walks or meals.
- Duration of the behaviour.
- Position in relation to the trainer – to the left and right, in front and behind, close and far away.
- Trainer position – standing, sitting on the floor, sitting in a chair
- Training set-up – treat bag or no treat bag, holding a treat in your hand or not.
- Environmental distractions – other people, other dogs, traffic, etc.

We can now draw up a detailed training plan for Jack (see page 57). Do remember that this is not set in stone and it could be completed successfully in a different order. For example, you might work on duration at each step, perhaps achieving 10 seconds before moving on to the next stage. Alternatively, you might train the full behaviour of hip to one side, and head on floor, before moving to a different environment. There is no one right or wrong way of proceeding as long as you are logical in the way in which you progress the criteria, and that you aim for successful repetitions as often as possible.

SAMPLE TRAINING PLAN

Behaviour	Location	Trainer Position
Hip to the right	Living Room	Sat on chair at dining table
Hip to the right	Living Room	Standing by dining table
Hip to the right	Living Room	Sat on sofa
Hip to the right	Living Room	Sat on floor
Hip to the right	Kitchen	Stood by oven
Hip to the right	Kitchen	Stood by door
Hip to the right	Bedroom	Sat on the bed
Hip to the right	Bedroom	Stood by the wardrobe
Hip to right and head to the floor	Living Room	Sat on chair at dining table
Hip to right and head to the floor, 3 sec duration	Living Room	Sat on chair at dining table
Hip to right and head to the floor, 5 sec duration	Living Room	Sat on chair at dining table
Hip to right and head to the floor, 10 second duration	Living Room	Sat on chair at dining table
Hip to right and head to the floor, 20 second duration	Living Room	Sat on chair at dining table
Hip to right and head to the floor, 3 sec duration	Living Room	Standing by dining table
Hip to right and head to the floor, 10 sec duration	Living Room	Standing by dining table
Hip to right and head to the floor, 20 sec duration	Living Room	Standing by dining table
Hip to right and head to the floor, 20 sec duration	Living Room	Sat on floor
Hip to right and head to the floor, 3 sec duration	Kitchen	Stood by door
Hip to right and head to the floor, 20 sec duration	Kitchen	Stood by door
Hip to right and head to the floor, 3 sec duration	Bedroom	Sat on bed
Hip to right and head to the floor, 20 sec duration	Bedroom	Sat on bed

Desensitisation

Once Jack can demonstrate the relaxed behaviour with duration, in a number of different places and with a range of distractions, then we can commence the desensitisation process. Now we can go back to our fear hierarchy which tells us that the very first stage, the one which Jack can cope with is a stranger walking past the garden gate.

With Jack having been cued to relax, we can set the scene for a stranger to walk past the gate. Brief your stranger what to do to ensure success, so that might include how fast to walk, whether Jack is given any eye contact and whether there is any pausing outside of the gate. Remember that we want Jack to be successful as often as possible, so we need to set the training up with that in mind at all times. It is much easier to commence at a very easy level and progress than to cause a fearful response and then try to compensate for it.

Cue Jack to relax and assess, are you still achieving the same level of relaxation as you saw within the training? If not, that's ok, it's just information that some training needs to be carried out within this particular set-up before commencing desensitisation.

If Jack can relax then we can ask our stranger to walk past the garden gate whilst we monitor Jack's body language and emotional state. Good level of relaxation? We can move on. Reduction in relaxation? Then we need to adjust our set-up. For example, the stranger could increase the distance between them and the gate as they walk past.

This becomes the process all the way through the desensitisation hierarchy, always trying to work at a level where we believe the dog can remain in a relaxed state whilst gradually exposing them to increasingly intense forms of the very thing which has caused the fear response.

Remember that your hierarchy and training plans were just starting points and it's highly likely that once you commence the process that you will gather more information about the dog and how they respond. In turn you will then need to adapt the plans to meet the needs of the individual dog.

As the process is likely to take place over a number of training sessions, keeping accurate records becomes essential. Making a note of what the last successful criteria was along with the environmental conditions – such as weather, distractions and time of day – can all be extremely useful when tracking progress or identifying common factors should the training not progress as expected. Children playing next door or an early morning session rather than in the evening might stall training for some dogs and having a note of these makes it quick to identify areas that may need some extra generalisation.

Limitations

One of the limitations of desensitisation is that the dog does not develop an emotional reaction to the feared situation other than a neutral relaxed state. In order for a positive association to be developed, systematic desensitisation is usually combined with counterconditioning. This involves associating the feared thing with something good, such as a treat, so that in turn it begins to predict good things for the dog. Do carefully consider whether you need a neutral response or a positive response. If you are not sure, this is discussed in more detail in Chapter 7: Counter Conditioning.

Desensitisation is also a reversible process, which means that sensitisation, the process which caused the fear to begin with, can reoccur.

Careful management of the environment is needed whilst the process of systematic desensitisation is underway. Within the case study for example, it would be important that Jack is not present when any strangers enter the house until he has successfully achieved that stage of the fear hierarchy.

As you will have seen within the case study, systematic desensitisation is not a quick process. This has then led to owner compliance being cited as a problem. Clear guidance is needed as to the importance of developing that strong foundation on which the process will sit if the technique is to be successful.

7 COUNTER-CONDITIONING

This chapter includes background information on the technique of counter-conditioning and a case study to demonstrate how the protocol can be applied. It concludes with a discussion on the limitations of the approach to help you decide if this might be an appropriate technique to use with a fearful dog.

BACKGROUND

Counter-conditioning involves the use of Pavlovian conditioning to reverse the unwanted effects of prior conditioning. That prior conditioning tells us that something has happened which now causes the dog to respond in a fearful way. Maybe it was a man wearing a baseball cap who startled the dog, which now results in fear towards anyone who happens to be wearing the same type of headwear. Perhaps he was bitten by a small white dog, which now causes a fearful response towards all dogs of the same type.

Mary Cover Jones, an American Psychologist, was the first to demonstrate the effectiveness of counter-conditioning. In 1924 she published details of her experiment entitled *Laboratory Study of Fear: The Case of Peter*.

Peter was a young child who was fearful of white rats and related items, such as white rabbits, feathers, and a fur rug. Mary began the counter-conditioning process with the rabbit, which caused the greatest fear. Starting with the rabbit at a distance of 3.5m (12ft), Peter was given his favourite food – candy. The rabbit was then brought closer and closer until it was nibbling Peter's fingers, and he was showing no sign of fear. The response evoked by the 'frightening' rabbit had now been replaced by one associated with receiving something highly prized – the candy.

When using counter-conditioning, it usually means changing the environmental set-up so that the dog begins to experience a positive emotional response rather than one of fear. It is often described as changing an undesirable behaviour to a desirable behaviour, but we need to be careful here. If a dog is fearful of something, to him, at that moment in time, the fearful behaviour is desirable. The undesirability is our interpretation of the response. We consider that having a dog that barks at people wearing baseball caps, or at small white dogs, to be undesirable. To the fearful dog, it makes perfect sense to ward off the very thing that causes him to feel fear.

This brings us to the point of understanding that counter-conditioning is not about addressing the demonstration of the fear, so by that I mean the outward physical signs of fear seen in the dog's body language. Instead it is about changing the dog's emotional response, which, in turn, will reduce the likelihood of him demonstrating those behaviours which we deem to be undesirable.

It is also useful to consider the difference between counter-conditioning and systematic desensitisation. Both processes are designed to change an unwanted response. However, systematic desensitisation results in a learned fear being extinguished by exposing the dog to the feared thing, so gradually, that he never feels the need to show that emotional response. In counter-conditioning, the unwanted response is not just extinguished; it is replaced by a new, opposite response.

We, therefore, then need to consider if the outcome of counter-conditioning is what we really want. For example, if a dog is fearful of bikes, do we want the dog to associate their presence with great things happening, such as the appearance of treats? We know it's not going to take many repetitions before the dog begins to get excited when he sees a bike because he has learnt that a bike means treats. Perhaps, instead, it would be better to have a dog who ignores the presence of bikes because

the fear has been extinguished through systematic desensitisation.

IN PRACTICE

To look at counter-conditioning in action, we are going to examine the case of Reg, a young crossbreed, who has become fearful of his harness being put on to go out for a walk. The background to the situation is that, just as the harness was being put on, there was a loud clap of thunder. Reg connected the thunder with what was happening at that exact moment in time – the harness being put on. Since that point, he became fearful even when he saw his owner picking up the harness.

In this situation, it was assessed that it would be fine for Reg to become excited when seeing the harness, a predictor for going out for a walk, which Reg enjoys. So, it was decided that counter-conditioning would be a good option.

THE FEAR HIERARCHY

Just as with systematic desensitisation, we can design a fear hierarchy. This helps us to consider where Reg is, right now, and where we hope he will be at the end of the counter-conditioning process. This hierarchy is all about the location of the harness. So first of all, we need to consider where the harness needs to be to allow Reg's fear to either be non-existent or so low that he still becomes excited when he sees his treats appear. While this is key to the process, the focus is on Reg's emotional state rather than celebrating that he ate a treat in the presence of the harness. We don't want to see is a dog who is such a 'foody' that he will still take the treats despite being very fearful. This may result in us using flooding instead of counter-conditioning. *See Chapter Twelve for details on the flooding technique and the risks associated with its use.*

So, to err on the side of safety, let's start with the harness in a neutral location, where we know Reg will be fear free. In this way, we will quickly move through the stages rather than having to take steps back down the hierarchy.

So for Reg, the first step in the hierarchy is having the harness hanging on the coat rack and our final step, for this part of the plan, is to be able to hold the harness by his shoulder. Progressing from this stage to wearing the harness will form the increments of a second plan.

Do remember that a plan is just that. Sometimes we can create a detailed plan and find that we can skip a few stages as the dog responds much more quickly than we expected. In other cases, we might need to break a stage down into multiple components.

For example, in Reg's case, holding the harness 60cm (2ft) from him may be fine, but a distance of 30cm (1ft) causes concern. Therefore, we need to introduce some extra stages to get from 60cm to 30cm. Careful and considered study of the dog's emotional state, and

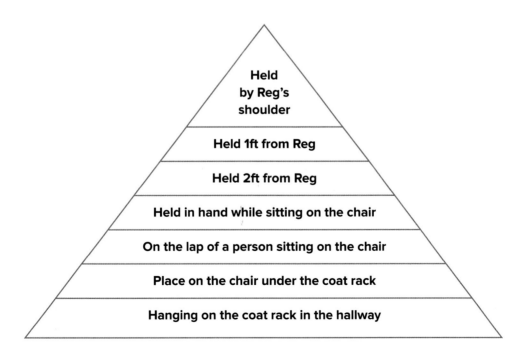

body language, throughout the process will quickly tell us how to progress or when we need to reduce the criteria.

Unlike systematic desensitisation, there is no relaxation protocol to teach, but there are three factors to consider before we get started:

1. Management while counter-conditioning

In Reg's case, we cannot use the harness to take him out for a walk until the counter-conditioning process is complete. If we insist that he wears it, we are going to cause fear, and that will take the process right back to the beginning each time. We also run the risk that the fear will intensify and generalise to other aspects of the 'getting ready for a walk' routine. So, for Reg, we are going to use a collar and lead rather than a harness. We are going to get ready for a walk inside the house rather than in the garden – and we are going to check the weather forecast for any predictions of thunder!

It would be great if there were some fixed rules around how far we need to take this new routine, but each dog will have his very own degree of generalisation of fear responses. Focussed observation of the dog's body language, and emotional responses, through careful exposure will tell us what is right for each individual dog. For some, using the same lead will be fine – maybe just using a different type of harness? For others, the whole 'getting ready for a walk' routine will need to be changed, or even put on hold, while the counter-conditioning process is undertaken. There are considerable benefits in our dogs having regular walks, but if they cause a fearful response, that benefit is lost. Assuming there is a garden where the dog can relieve himself, it may be possible to provide enrichment activities as an alternative to a walk while the counter-conditioning process is underway. *Take a look at Chapter Four: Welcoming a Fearful Dog into Your Home for some enrichment ideas.*

2. Planning the counter-conditioning session

In training and behaviour work, it is essential to consider both the logistics of the process, and our own mechanical skills, i.e. how we physically carry out the counter-conditioning process. This will include how the scary item is presented, and the delivery of the counter-conditioning food.

Firstly, we should consider how to get the scary item into, and out of, position without over-exposing the dog. Then we need to work how to deliver the high-value treat so that it does not encourage the dog to come closer to the harness purely because he desperately wants the food, despite being fearful of it. When this happens, you will see the dog edging closer to the food, grabbing it, and then quickly backing off. This is not what we are looking for in counter-conditioning.

This level of planning and practice – without the dog being present – reduces the risk of mistakes, which may escalate the fear. For example, In Reg's case, if the harness swoops in close beside him as it is moved into position, it may just confirm his perception that it is both scary and unpredictable.

3. Deciding on the good thing

Referring back to Peter and the rabbit (see page 59), bear in mind that Peter was given his favourite candy as the rabbit was moved, progressively, closer to him. If that candy had been swapped for a piece of dry bread, it is highly unlikely that Mary Cover Jones would have achieved the same result. It's also important to note that Peter did not approach the rabbit to get the candy; the candy was given to Peter as the rabbit was moved, progressively, closer to him.

With counter-conditioning, we are looking for transference. That means the excitement from getting something fantastic transfers to the scary thing. So, we need to find something good – something that ignites immediate excitement. The likely candidates are going to be treats, such as cheese or cooked chicken, but it can be anything your dog loves. Most dogs get just as excited over a small piece of cheese as they do over a large piece so, to avoid digestive issues, the pieces should be

big enough to taste but small enough so as not to require much chewing. In all likelihood we are going to complete several repetitions, within a training session, so we don't want the dog to become full, or for the food to lose its appeal.

We also need to think about how easy it is to deliver the treats. For example, thin, sliced ham tends to stick together, and so can be fiddly to give, resulting in delays during the counter-conditioning process. Try out a food type in advance, away from the scary thing. Check out how easy it is to work with – and make sure the dog thinks it's a great choice too!

THE COUNTER-CONDITIONING PROCESS

We now have a plan for each of the stages we will move through. We have great treats, and we have considered, and practised, the logistics. Now we are ready to start the counter-conditioning process.

We are now going to follow the steps in the fear hierarchy (see page 61) which have been designed to help Reg with his fear of the harness being close to him.

First stage: Harness hanging on the coat rack in the hallway

The harness needs to be positioned, and the treats organised – all cut up and ready to go. We need to ensure that Reg knows the location of the harness so we can bring him into the area, touch the harness and, at the same time, give him a treat.

Remember that we are not rewarding an excited response. Instead, we are building a connection between 'touch the harness' and receiving great food. There is no requirement for the dog to do anything to receive the food. If we were to go down the route of training a physical response, such as he must show calm behaviour to get the food, we may find that the dog can demonstrate the physical behaviour, yet still be experiencing a fearful emotion.

Over several repetitions, we are likely to see emergence of physical responses when we touch the harness. These might include looking towards us in anticipation or jumping up to get the food. However, these are not criteria that must be met in order for the food to be given.

As we repeat touching the harness, and giving the treat, we need to observe the dog's body language the whole time. Our assessment of his emotional state then provides us with two options:

1. If the dog is showing positive emotional responses and, remember, this is excitement that results from seeing the harness being touched because he knows that food will follow, then we can progress to the next stage.

2. If we are not getting positive emotional responses from touching the harness and, remember, that's the purpose of counter-conditioning applied in this way, then we need to reduce the criteria. So, the first step may be to point towards the harness and then, step-by-step, move your hand closer and closer until it makes contact.

The dog will convey how he is feeling about the set-up so observe his emotional responses closely to help judge the criteria. When the fear of the scary item is sufficiently low enough, or absent, the excitement response can emerge.

For Reg the remaining stages, which then take us to the point of the harness being held by his shoulder, are all carried out in exactly the same way.

LIMITATIONS

One key limitation of counter-conditioning, as I have mentioned previously, is whether you really want an excited response to the formerly scary thing. A more neutral response may be more appropriate. It was fine for Reg to get excited at seeing his harness, but a dog becoming excited when a car passes, or when a man with a walking stick strolls by, is less likely to be the outcome that we are looking for.

We need to be able to set up the situation reliably and to avoid the dog coming into contact with the scary thing during the counter-conditioning process. So, something like a fear of thunder may be challenging to counter-condition for the following reasons:

- There are very few repetitions to work with.
- We cannot control the intensity in order to work through a fear hierarchy.
- It may be challenging to predict exactly when the scary thing – the thunder – is going to happen.

This chapter includes background information on the technique of habituation followed by a case study to demonstrate how the protocol can be applied.

It concludes with a discussion on the limitations of habituation to help you decide if this might be an appropriate technique to use with a fearful dog.

Habituation results in a response to a stimulus gradually reducing when it is repeatedly presented, increasing the threshold. In plain English, that means that you just 'get used to it'. Habituation is considered to be the simplest, most universal form of learning and is known to take place in species ranging from a one-cell organism right through to us humans.

For habituation to take place, there needs to be a repeated response, which then weakens. Thinking about how this takes place in day-to-day life, imagine living in the country but taking a holiday in the city. On the first few nights, the noise of traffic means you toss and turn and struggle to sleep. But, come maybe the third or fourth night, you get to sleep a little easier, but it still takes much longer than if you were at home. By day five, you barely notice the background noise, and you sleep soundly. Note that there was no gradual increase in the volume of traffic to help you adjust – you just 'got used to it'.

Although we usually associate habituation with emotions, there can also be an orienting response. Imagine a dog hears a new sound; not only does he stop what he is doing, he is also likely to turn his head and prick up his ears. If the sound is repeated several times and is of no consequence to the dog, then that orientating response will begin to disappear.

Habituation allows us, and our dogs, to ignore repetitive and irrelevant information, thus freeing up the resources that enable us to be responsive to new and changing details. If we were constantly aware of everything that is happening around us, it would be difficult to get anything done or even to relax.

THE FEATURES OF HABITUATION

The decline in response through habituation is considered to be temporary. So if you go back to your countryside home, and do not return to the city for another year, the chances are that the startle response will reappear as strongly as it did the first time. This resurgence is often discussed as spontaneous recovery; you thought you had extinguished the response, but it was there lurking in the background ready to reappear.

Another feature to consider is the length of exposure to the stimulus. Imagine moving home and finding that the noise from a children's park is almost constant throughout the day. The consistent presence of the stimulus allows the habituation process to take place quickly, and soon you barely notice the sound of the children playing. If, however, the children living next door have friends across to play once a week, you may still be disturbed by the sound several months later.

Predictability also plays a part in whether habituation takes place. If you are at a firework display, you are probably expecting to hear some loud bangs, so you may be less likely to startle than if a firework went off without warning.

Habituation is also affected by what is called over-learning. This is learning that takes place even if the response to a stimulus has completely disappeared. It is sometimes called below-zero habituation because it happens when there is no apparent response to

the stimulus. Imagine that you had a dog who was fearful of gunshot. After hearing 10 gunshots, his startle response completely disappears. The next day, the dog again shows a startle response when he hears gunshot. But if there had been 50 gunshots on the first day, the dog would probably show less of a startle response on the second day. So even though the additional 40 gunshots produced no change in the dog's behaviour at the time, they did increase the long-term retention of the habituation.

Generalisation can happen within habituation. So, if a few days later, there are more gunshots but they sound a little different – perhaps different types of guns – the dog may give them little attention. The amount of generalisation that takes place would, however, depend on how similar the new sound is compared to the habituated sound.

The intensity of the stimulus is another consideration in whether or not habituation can take place.

Imagine being on holiday in the city; there is a car parked close by and its alarm goes off several times each evening. The noise is so shrill that it still causes you to startle several days later. You never get to the point of habituation, even by the end of your week's holiday. Instead of habituation, sensitisation has taken place.

SENSITISATION

Sensitisation occurs when there is either a repeated, or single, intense exposure to a stimulus resulting in the increasing intensity of the response. Imagine you are at work, and your boss comes over and loudly berates you for making a mistake. You feel angry and embarrassed because he reprimanded you in front of everyone in the office. The next day he walks out of his office and heads in your direction. You start to feel nervous, and your heart rate increases even though he walks straight past you. That single, intense exposure was enough to cause the sensitisation process and create both an emotional and physiological response.

Sensitisation can also happen over several repetitions of the stimulus. For example, your dog is happily mooching around in the garden and, suddenly, the dog from next door comes running up to the fence and barks at him. He is likely to react with a startle response and then an emotional response, such as barking back. Over a couple of days, this happens a few more times. Then you begin to notice a change in your dog's behaviour, which has taken place through the sensitisation process.

Firstly, he is now looking for predictors of the threat. So, as he goes out into the garden, he looks over to the fence line suspiciously. Then with ears flat and tail tucked, he furtively stares in that direction as he walks past. Even if the other dog doesn't appear, your dog still goes through this behaviour routine just in case, because this is his preparation strategy, which then allows him to cope with the situation.

We can see that sensitisation is about survival. Becoming aware of potentially dangerous situations, and taking action to keep safe, makes perfect sense. However, the process of sensitisation does not result in a fixed outcome. This means the emotion that has been developed can be replaced with a different response. To do this, we can use techniques such as desensitisation (see Chapter Six) and counter-conditioning (see Chapter Seven).

THE LEARNING THEORY

Habituation is an example of non-associative learning. This means that the behaviour changes without the presence of any apparent, associated reinforcement or punishment. For example, the reduction in a puppy's response to the washing machine is not because he has been reinforced with a treat each time the machine was switched on and he remained calm. Nor has he been punished for showing anxiety.

Now this is why there can be resistance from some behaviourists, who claim that habituation is not, in fact, a learning process. That is because learning requires the development of a response, whereas habituation is all about a reduction in response. However, it could be argued that learning is about a change in behaviour due to experience, and that is precisely what happens within habituation.

As to why it takes place – well, there are several theories, but two are most frequently cited:

- **Single-factor theory of habituation:** The constant repetition of the stimulus changes its effect. Our brains no longer give it attention; we have, in effect, become bored by it.
- **Dual-factor theory of habituation:** This theory suggests that there are processes underway within our brains that are responsible for regulating how we respond to different stimuli. So, in relation to the puppy's response to the washing machine, he makes a decision to ignore it because there are more important things that require his attention.

There can sometimes be confusion in identifying the difference between habituation and extinction. Even though we know that they are processed within largely overlapping circuits in the brain, there is a crucial difference. Within extinction, we withdraw the reinforcement, which was previously sustaining the behaviour. For example, if we no longer reinforce a dog for jumping up, that behaviour may gradually weaken until it no longer happens, resulting in its extinction. Within habituation, there is no reinforcement to withdraw.

APPLYING THE TECHNIQUE

When we consider the application of habituation, we most often associate it with young pups. Their world is full of new things to habituate to: the washing machine, the television, the lawnmower, the list goes on and on. Generally, it all happens seamlessly. There may be some initial curiosity, but mostly the pup will habituate towards the stimulus over a period of time. Great! We need to do nothing. But how do we know whether the puppy is going to habituate or sensitise to a new stimulus? Well, the risk of habituation or sensitisation will vary with each dog. The dog's individual personality, and his emotional state at the time, may both influence the outcome.

The characteristics of the stimulus will also play a part. A sudden, very loud bang is probably going to cause a more significant negative emotional response compared to the noise of a continually dripping tap. This is where careful planning is needed, when you need to think about the individual dog and consider the likelihood of him 'spooking' at something new. If in doubt, play it safe and plan a desensitisation or counter-conditioning process when you introduce a new, potentially scary, thing. You may find that the dog shows little emotional response and so you can whizz through the stages of your plan super quick. Or you may find that you were right in your concerns but your diligence means you have successfully avoided the development of a fearful response.

DISHABITUATION

If you start responding to a stimulus, once more, after previously habituating towards it, then it may be because of what is called dishabituation. When we habituate, we stop paying attention until something changes, and we then respond with new interest.

So if you suddenly begin to notice the sound of a dripping tap when you had become habituated to it weeks before, it might be because the drip has become more frequent. If your fearful dog had habituated towards the sound of the television but suddenly there was a horror movie, with loud and dramatic noise, he might experience dishabituation.

THE HABITUATION CONTEXT

When you have, or are working with, a fearful dog and you are contemplating habituation as a strategy, the consistency

and complexity of the environment must be considered.

A consistent environment can be reassuring to a fearful dog. A place for everything, and everything in its place, reduces the need to scan for potentially scary things. However, when the environment is always the same, but you then need to introduce change, you may need to carry out some careful planning before it is introduced.

The complexity of the environment also needs to be assessed. Imagine an anxious dog entering the house only to come across the sound of a new washing machine on its spin cycle. While it may cause an initial startle response, habituation may quickly follow. But if, in addition to the sound and vibrations of the washing machine, there is a new vacuum cleaner in the corner of the room, then the change to the environment may be too much to cope with. Rather than habituation taking place, you now have sensitisation to both the washing machine and vacuum cleaner.

This complexity could also apply to being in a new setting. The fearful dog may have habituated to the noise of the vacuum in the kitchen, but that doesn't mean there won't be a startle response when you first move it to the living room. In addition, the habituation may only be specific to that particular vacuum cleaner, so should you buy a new one, you may find the change in appearance, aroma, and sound requires a new process of habituation. Now many dogs can generalise their previous life experiences to new situations. So, despite some differences between the two vacuums, there may be enough familiar characteristics, and contextual cues, to allow the dog to quickly move towards habituation.

You can then see from this that understanding, and assessing, the individual dog is essential when considering habituation as a strategy for fearful responses. For some, that vacuum can be moved all around the house, and it will cause little reaction. For others, the process of habituation may never result in 'getting used to it'.

IN PRACTICE

To look at habituation in practice, let's take the case of Chloe and Sam, two Border Collies who had grown up in a busy, urban environment. Their owner, Sue, had been the perfect puppy owner, carefully going through a process of socialisation when they were young, attending a rewards-based puppy class with each one, and ensuring that they had positive experiences in a wide range of environments.

When they were two years old, Sue got a new job which took her to live in rural North Yorkshire. There she and the dogs quickly got used to a quieter way of life, and they enjoyed spending hours wandering across the Dales.

Three years later, Sue moved back to her former home. This was when she got in touch to book a behavioural consultation.

The Issues

Both Chloe and Sam had become terrified of the heavy traffic near their home. They needed to walk alongside the busy road to get to a field where they could run off lead. In the video that Sue sent to me, I could see that Chloe was worst affected. She walked crouched low to the ground, and when a vehicle went past, she froze. After two or three cars going by, Chloe was frantic and could not be consoled by Sue, with whom she usually had an excellent and trusting relationship.

Sam also showed signs of fear, though not to the same extent as Chloe, but Sue was concerned that he was becoming worse over time.

To avoid the issue, Sue had begun walking the dogs very early in the morning when there was little traffic around.

Evaluation

When I met the dogs, both were very relaxed and happy to show me their extensive repertoire of behaviours. Chatting about the issue, Sue couldn't think of anything that had happened to cause the fearful response. The only change had been in environment, moving from urban to rural, and then back to urban.

Going back a little further, Sue explained that when the dogs were first walked in traffic, as puppies, they had both been worried. Over a few weeks that reaction lessened which led Sue to believe that habituation had taken place. However, the important aspect here is that it had decreased. The dogs had not stopped responding when exposed to the stimulus. This caused me to question whether habituation had taken place, or whether the dogs were simply coping in the best way they could.

When they were reintroduced to the heavy traffic after time away, sensitisation had occurred.

The Plan

Attempting to habituate the dogs to the traffic was not an option. In this situation, it was far more likely that flooding would take place. Therefore, the plan was for Sue and the dogs to go through a process of desensitisation. This started with the relaxation process, which the dogs leant in the home, and then generalised in the front garden, which leads to the road.

From there, the dogs spent time watching the traffic from the gate. At this point, Sue suggested asking the dogs to offer some of their well-known

and reinforced behaviours. The logic being that this would build a positive association with the road. While this sounds as if it might be a good idea, there is a risk that the fear may be masked by the dogs' keenness to offer the behaviour. This would make it difficult to see if there was any residual fear when deciding to progress the desensitisation plan to the next stage.

Once the dogs were showing calm and relaxed behaviour while they were watching the traffic, Sue was, finally, able to walk them for a few paces, on the pavement, as the traffic went by.

Outcome

Three months from starting the plan, Sue reported that they were now taking occasional walks by the busy road. Chloe was still aware of the traffic, but her body language was much more relaxed than previously. She was also able to listen to Sue and respond to her cues. Sam, meanwhile, was showing no signs of fear.

Summary

Sometimes we are not always doing what we think we are. It may have looked as if Chloe and Sam were habituating to the traffic when they were puppies but, in reality, that process was not taking place. Instead, both dogs were coping with the traffic situation. Therefore, habituation was not the right process to use to help the dogs to cope with the traffic on their return to urban life. Instead, a programme of desensitisation was used. This allowed the dogs' responses to the stimuli to be carefully monitored and resulted in a successful outcome.

LIMITATIONS: TOLERANCE OR HABITUATION?

Tolerance is seen when a dog appears to cope with a situation, but body language and demeanour tells you that he is far from 'getting used to it'.

When you switch on the washing machine, does the dog continue to relax in the kitchen, or does he get up and leave the room? What if the doors are closed, and the dog is unable to leave the room? Now he has to tolerate the noise, which he finds, at best, unpleasant.

There are times when we all have to tolerate things that we find annoying, unpleasant, or which cause a little anxiety. But for a fearful dog, there is the risk of what is called trigger stacking.

A trigger is something that is added to the environment, which then causes an increase in a dog's awareness, fear, or reactivity. When there is a combination, or series of triggers, they build up as layers until they create a tipping point.

So, let's imagine a morning for our fearful dog:

- Neighbours cut the grass with a noisy strimmer.
- Children on bikes come too close during the morning walk.
- While the owner goes shopping, the dog is left in a room with the washing machine switched on.

Our fearful dog has learnt to tolerate each of these scenarios in isolation but, this morning, they have been stacking up. Now when the owner returns home with a friend who our dog hasn't met before, he is pushed over the limit of his tolerance.

In isolation, our dog could cope with each of the four triggers; he might even be able to cope with three out of the four. But when all four occur – one after another – without the time to drop back down to calmness, it became just too much.

A behaviourist often has to play detective in this type of situation. When the client calls to say that they have had a setback, we need to understand the full context of what has happened. We can then identify those triggers, which may explain why the dog could not cope with the new person coming into the home.

So how do we cope with situations that our dog tolerates but has not habituated to? Well, management of the environment may be one option. That means that the washing machine only goes on when the dog has the opportunity to move to another room. When new people are expected, we engineer the time before their arrival to be as calm as possible for our dog.

Desensitisation (see Chapter Six) may be an option if we can have some control over the fear-inducing situation to allow for gentle introductions. Counter-conditioning (see Chapter Seven) could be another approach for when we are looking to reverse the fear response to an opposite emotion.

THE TARGETED APPROACH PROTOCOL

In this chapter, I introduce the Targeted Approach Protocol (TAP), starting with background information on how it came to be developed along with the procedure for its use in assisting fearful dogs. This is followed by a case study of TAP in action and then a discussion of its limitations.

BACKGROUND

The Targeted Approach Protocol developed from research I undertook for my MSc in Applied Animal Behaviour and Training. At the time, I was living close to the Galgos del Sol Rescue (GDS) in the Murcia region of Spain. This is a wonderful organisation that always has over 150 Galgos and Podenco in their kennels, at any one time, as well as a long waiting list for these noble hunting dogs to come into their care.

If you are not familiar with this type of dog, think Greyhound-shape, but with the understanding that they are different breeds. The Galgos tend to have a sweet, forgiving nature while the Podenco has an inquisitive and mischievous side to their personality. They are both popular hunting breeds in Spain but, sadly, they are subject to so much abuse and neglect that there is a never-ending stream of dogs

abandoned, or needing rescue from unimaginable squalor.

Once in the care of GDS, the majority of the dogs quickly come to realise that people can be the source of tender care and very positive experiences. However, for a small number of dogs, their experiences have been so traumatic that they have deep-seated fears of any human contact. These are dogs who cannot eat in front of people, who hide at the back of their kennels and who urinate in fear if someone comes too close.

With those responses in mind, it is easy to see that many of the approaches we would usually adopt with a fearful dog are not going to be suitable. So this was the situation that resulted in the Targeted Approach Protocol. I wanted a way in which I could interact with these dogs, giving them as much choice as possible, while slowly developing trust.

PROCEDURES

TAP involves using a target which the dog is reinforced for interacting with. I use 'free shaping' meaning that I look for, mark, and reinforce, behaviours which lead towards achieving my goal — in this case interacting with a cone. Free shaping is generally associated with using a clicker to mark the correct behaviours. However, within TAP, it is important to assess each dog as to how he responds to the use of a clicker sound and whether a marker word would be more effective. Targeting requires the dog to touch a specific object (the cone), usually with his paw or nose. This works well with fearful dogs for three reasons:

1. The trainer can be some distance away.
2. The dog can choose to target.
3. Many dogs, even those who are fearful, are curious about new objects.

The key aim of using targeting within TAP is not about how quickly we get the behaviour, it's about providing a consistent and reliable sequence of events which are under the dog's control and which allow the trust to develop.

It is also not about luring. When I was presenting this technique at a conference, a delegate suggested that I could place food on the object, and that would get the targeting behaviour much more quickly. However, when we add a lure, many dogs become so obsessed with the food that they tentatively edge forward to reach it, and then quickly retreat. By doing this, we increase the fear that they are experiencing through their desire for the food and, as a result, we place them in a situation of turmoil. They do want the food, but they don't want to come closer to the person or environment, which is causing fear. When you see that 'grab and run' response, it means that, rather than increasing trust, we have increased uncertainty.

When using TAP, I always work on a schedule of continuous reinforcement, so that means every time the dog offers a behaviour, he is reinforced. Remember, this is about building trust and consistency; the dog offers the behaviour and then he gets reinforced, every single time.

There is no need for a visual or verbal cue, so that means no pointing or telling the dog to "touch" for example. The presence of the cone will become an environmental cue. So when the cone is there, the dog learns that if he interacts, he will get reinforced. This means that the process is under the dog's control. He is never placed in a situation where he follows a cue even though it puts him in a position where he feels apprehensive or fearful.

What you need

When I am conducting a TAP session, I generally, use a small sports cone for the target for the following reasons:
- It's easy and cheap to buy.
- Most pet dogs have never previously interacted with one.
- If it's knocked over, it doesn't make a loud, scary noise.
- It's large enough to be very obvious to the dog when it is placed in a room.

I also make sure I have a good supply of suitable food rewards. I need treats which are of sufficient weight, to throw away from me; I don't want the dog to have to come closer to me in order to reach them. I strongly suggest that you practise with different treats and hone your motor skills, so you are able to throw with reasonable accuracy before you begin.

TAP IN ACTION FOR SITUATIONAL FEAR

Step-by-step

1. The client places the cone in the room approximately one metre (3ft) from the dog.
2. I look for any attention, including eye contact, directed at the cone. I mark and reinforce with a treat thrown towards the cone.
3. After five minutes or ten clicks – whichever comes first – the session ends by the dog and client leaving the room. I lift the cone from the floor once they have left.
4. When the client and dog return, the client, once again, places the cone one metre from the dog.

Setting the foundations

Typically, we cycle through steps 1-3, three times in a session. Leaving the room and then coming back in, provides me with the opportunity to assess what understanding has developed. For example, when the dog and client re-enter the room, and the cone is placed in position, I calculate how long it takes for the dog to interact with the cone and receive his first reinforcement.

Before moving on to the next step, I am looking for evidence of understanding. I want to be confident that the dog knows that if he looks at, or touches, the cone, then good stuff is coming his way.

In the first stages of using TAP, I mark the dog's interaction with the cone and throw the treat rather than asking the client to be the trainer. The reason for this is that few clients have the mechanical skills to be able to accurately mark the behaviour in the early stages. If you are an experienced 'shaper', then you will be skilled in observing behaviour and will be able to notice and mark the smallest glance in the direction of the cone. It is essential that the dog be consistently, and accurately, reinforced to start the process.

Once the dog reaches the 'got-it' moment, and has a history of reinforcement in place, we can practise the mechanics of the process without the dog. I take on the canine role, approaching and touching the cone so that the client can perfect their timing, and treat delivery, before working with their own dog. Once these skills are established, the client can follow TAP without additional help.

I am a strong believer in keeping records of training sessions. It allows me to accurately assess the dog's developing understanding of the behaviour and to carefully, and methodically, increase the criteria. I also find that it provides a really useful way for the client to assess how their dog is progressing, especially on days when things don't seem to be going to plan!

Ways to assess understanding and progress include:

- Measuring the time it takes for the first interaction with the cone to take place.
- Measuring the time between interactions with the cone.
- Assessing the dog's confidence when he is targeting.

Moving to generalisation

The key to TAP is the complete predictability for the dog, compared to a world where there has been uncertainty and instability. So once the dog is showing that he 'gets it', we can begin generalising the behaviour. That means going through the same process but in lots of different settings and environments.

This is the step which clients are tempted to skip through as quickly as possible. But we are building a foundation here; a foundation on which we can begin to work on the causes of the fear. If that foundation isn't strong

enough, it will crumble when placed under pressure.

So we are, therefore, looking for the dog's ability to target the cone in several different locations and set-ups before using it in the setting which causes a fearful response.

For a dog who is fearful of getting into a car, that might mean working through three more training sessions in each of the following locations:

1. Living room
2. Kitchen
3. Bedroom
4. Garden
5. Bathroom
6. Front of car
7. Left-hand side of the car
8. Right-hand side of the car
9. Rear of car
10. The rear of the car with the boot open
11. Inside the car with boot open
12. Inside the car with boot open and engine running
13. Inside the car with the boot closed
14. Inside the car with the boot closed and engine running

Now, that looks as if it's going to take an awfully long time to finally get to the point of the dog getting into the car, having the boot closed and the engine running. However, when I talk with clients and ask them how long they have been experiencing the problem, it's usually several months and in some cases, several years. So that is why I ask them to invest a few more months of working with their dog to finally move forward.

WHERE TAP WORKS BEST

When I first conducted my research with the Galgos and Podenco in Spain, I found that TAP was most effective with those dogs who demonstrated the far extremes of fear. In the presence of people and the cone, these formerly extremely fearful dogs began to spend more time in the middle of their kennel run rather than hiding at the back. There was also some predictability about interactions with people.

For dogs with moderate fear, I found that desensitisation and counter-conditioning worked equally well. It is essential to recognise that TAP is not going to be the right approach for every dog and every situation. However, the protocol provides you with another 'tool for the box' should you come across a case where other techniques seem too advanced.

Over the last few years, I have been using TAP as a technique within my behavioural consultations, and there are two key situations where the approach has provided good levels of success:

1. **To restore confidence in a situation which has created fear.** I have now worked on several cases where a dog has developed a fear of getting into a car. Sometimes this has been after a traumatic experience, such as an accident, resulting in sensitisation. In other cases, the dog has never found car travelling to be a positive experience resulting in a gradual development of the fear until it becomes overwhelming.

2. **To restore confidence in people or a specific person.** In some cases, this has happened accidentally. For example, one very sensitive dog became extremely fearful of a member of the family who had thrown a toy, which then, accidentally, caught the dog on the head. In another case, a dog who had been rescued from a puppy farm environment, had never experienced positive human interaction and mistrusted all the efforts of her new family to bond with her.

The approach also requires that the dog is sufficiently inquisitive to investigate a new object. To assess this, I ask clients what normally happens when they introduce a new toy. For TAP to be a possibility, the dog does not need to immediately play with the toy, or even be overly excited, but he does need to show some curiosity so that, at a minimum, he will look towards it.

TAP provides an opportunity to commence the rehabilitation process. Once you have established a degree of trust with the dog through TAP, it's likely that you will be able to move on to other techniques. The approach has proved to be successful in reaching dogs, who seem to be so off-the-scale in terms of their fear, that it leaves staff at rescue centres and owners wondering if they will ever be able to gain trust. In each of the behavioural cases I have worked on, using TAP, the owners have tried other methods without success.

We know that context shapes future expectations of similar experiences so that means that the consistency of TAP can be transferred to other situations. For the dog, that means the presence of the cone always gives the same result, the freedom to act without pressure.

TAP IN ACTION

I mentioned earlier a case where a very sensitive dog had become extremely fearful of a member of the family who had thrown a toy which had then accidentally caught the dog on the head. In this case, it was a 10-year-old boy, Jack, who had become the source of the fear. Although the child interacted with the dog, his parents felt that Jess, the three-year-old Shetland Sheepdog, had never been overly fond of him. Jess was a rescue dog who had been with the new family for just over a year. It is highly likely that the toy-throwing incident was a 'final straw' for Jess – a confirmation in her mind as to why her mistrust of Jack was justified.

I could see that Jess was visibly fearful when Jack entered the room and she created distance between them

wherever possible. So, we decided to commence TAP while Jack was at school and that was for two reasons:

Firstly, it was to ensure that Jack, the cause of the fear, would not be present while we got Jess. There was no possibility of him walking in on a session.

Secondly, Jack was very upset about the situation and genuinely wanted to have a good relationship with Jess. Despite his desire to help, we didn't want him to attempt to undertake cone work by himself at this early stage.

Setting the Foundations

The process we followed was exactly the same as for the situational fear. We introduced the cone and then generalised the behaviour all around the house and garden until we had a very solid response, and Jess clearly demonstrated that she understood the game.

Jess proved to be a very enthusiastic student; she quickly understood the required targeting behaviour. In just over a week, she had generalised touching the cone with her nose in all the rooms of the house and in the garden. The next step was to see if Jess was able to continue offering the response when Jack was present.

The first time we introduced Jack to the process, we decided to work outside in the garden. Jack was asked to wait at the far end of the garden with Dad, while I stayed with Mum and Jess close to the house. This meant that Jess could leave the situation and go into the house if she wanted, and in so doing would not have to walk past Jack. Providing the dog with every opportunity to stay or leave is an essential part of TAP.

When working with treats, we do have to consider that their presence could be an inducement for some dogs to stay in the training environment despite feeling fear or anxiety. So that means that careful observation of body language is essential, as is noticing any grab and run type responses when a treat is thrown. On the flip side, the removal of the treats and, in this case, the cone, could also be very punishing to some dogs. In the case of Jess, we marked the end of a training session by offering her daily chew stick. This provided a transition which smoothed out the sudden unavailability of treats and the potential for frustration.

Introducing the feared stimulus – Jack! During the first session with Jack present, Jess decided to leave the garden and go into the house after just five repetitions of the targeting behaviour. We lifted the cone, returned to the house and decided that this would then provided us with a baseline for the next session; we would only reinforce a maximum of four targeting behaviours and then we would lift the cone and finish. Even when sessions don't go to plan, they have considerable value in providing you with information to guide the next training session.

The next session saw Jess successfully complete her four targets, and then we finished by giving her the chew stick.

Over a period of weeks, Jess targeted the cone in various environments with Jack present. In a new environment, we dropped the repetitions down to four, always making sure that the set-up allowed Jess to leave the session should she choose to.

After a month of training, we transferred the responsibility for marking the targeting behaviour to Jack; his timing was excellent, as I find so often to be the case with child trainers! Jess accepted this transition without any change in her emotional state and with no further episodes of leaving the training environment.

After a further week, Jack took on the role of treat delivery while Mum clicked. This was the stage where we had to take particular care of how the treat would be delivered; we wanted to ensure that there would be no potential for the treat to be thrown and hit Jess. The sensitisation that had happened many months ago, with the throwing of the toy, might just reappear in that situation.

So Jack practised throwing the treats low and aiming to get them on to a mat, which would be placed a short distance from Jess. After lots of practice, Jack could consistently throw the treat so that it flew through the air, low to the ground, and landed on the mat. We then had two sessions of Mum dropping the treat on the mat so that it became a reliable place for the reinforcement to be delivered, and then we introduced Jack as the treat delivery mechanism.

Jess couldn't have cared less! From here, the training sped on with Jack both clicking and treating. The key breakthrough came when Jack opened the cupboard to get the cone to start a session, and Jess came running excitedly into the room and jumped up on him with tail wagging. Finally, the process had enabled Jess to see Jack as a consistent and trustworthy person.

There was still some way to go to achieve the 'boy and his dog' relationship that Jack so desperately wanted, but a window of opportunity had opened. Now there was a foundation on which I could help the two of them to further deepen their relationship.

KEY POINTS ON USING TAP

TAP provides an inroad to achieving trust where other techniques are not suitable or have been unsuccessful. To be effective the practitioner must adhere to following points:

- Not to use lures or prompts when first training the targeting behaviour
- Not to add a verbal or visual cue – the cone becomes an environmental cue.
- Always ensure the dog has the opportunity to end or leave a session.
- Generalise the targeting behaviour thoroughly before introducing it to the fear-inducing scenario.

LIMITATIONS OF TAP

Whatever is causing the fear needs to be avoided during the process. So, if a dog has a fear of getting into cars, he should not go on car journeys until the process is completed. In the case of Jack and Jess, we could not remove Jack from Jess's environment entirely, but we asked Jack not to attempt to make friends with Jess in the short-term.

Ideally, the dog needs to be inquisitive around new objects. If this is not the case, it doesn't preclude the use of TAP, but it does mean you will need to shape the dog's behaviour towards the object to allow the targeting to take place.

Understanding how a dog touching a cone will result in greater confidence often requires a client to take a leap of faith. I have found that not all clients 'buy in' the start of the process, but if I can gain their commitment to giving it a go, it becomes an enjoyable game for both dog and owner. This alone has great benefits in relationship building.

Confidence grows in both dog and owner and a strong history of reinforcement is being developed. All of these aspects come together and develop a stronger base on which to transition the learning to the fear inducing scenario.

Development of the TAP technique

TAP is still a very new technique and I encourage trainers and owners who are interested in its application to get in touch for further help and advice. If you have successfully used the method, I would love to hear more and add the details to our portfolio of TAP case studies.

The use of medication in helping our dogs overcome fearful responses has, in the past, been a controversial choice. In this chapter I discuss how this perspective is changing. I have included descriptions of a range of medications and the circumstances for when they may be a helpful addition to a behaviour modification plan.

I also present my own dog, Fizz, as a case study, to illustrate how the use of medication helped him to overcome his fear of unknown people.

At one point, we would have considered a pharmacological option as a last resort for fearful dogs. However, as the use of human behavioural medicine has grown, so has the use of drugs to influence animal behaviour. Perceptions have also changed, and there is now much greater acceptance of drugs as an appropriate step in assisting with a dog's psychological distress.

That said, we should be aware that many drugs used within the treatment of behavioural issues are known as 'extra-label'. This means that they are being used in a way that is inconsistent with what is indicated on the label, usually because they have been developed for human use. The cost for manufacturers to bring those medications to market for common animal species is usually prohibitive, which leaves vets in the situation of having to consider 'extra-label' use.

The situations when 'extra-label' is considered to be suitable, varies from country to country but, typically, it may be:

- When there is no animal drug approved for the intended use.
- The required dosage, or concentration, is not available.

The veterinarian should warn the client of potential side effects and risks associated with the use of the drug and they may be asked to sign a consent form to allow the use of the medication for their dog.

Prior to medication being prescribed, the dog should undergo a full medical examination, which could include blood and urine testing, along with a thyroid panel. Further information on why these may be necessary can be found in Chapter 2: The Physiological Basis of Fear. However, you should be prepared to discuss the dog's case history in detail so the vet is able to consider which underlying neurochemical mechanisms are in play and can then prescribe appropriate medication.

Drugs, in combination with behaviour modification, can be used to manage challenging behaviour problems. These may be situations where there has been an insufficient response to non-pharmacological approaches, and the dog's health and welfare is impacted.

The aim of this approach is to open a window of opportunity through which learning can take place. The medication should not be administered to sedate the dog, or slow him down, as the issue – the fear – is still there and will remain unresolved when the effect of the medication wears off. That said, there may be emergencies where drugs can play a role in providing a short-term state of calm to help a dog cope with an unexpected situation and prevent further distress.

Within this chapter, medication options are discussed as either being daily meds or situational meds:

Daily meds form part of a long-term behaviour modification plan. They may have a subtle, and more gradual effect on the way in which a dog responds to fear-inducing situations.

Situational meds are those which are given only when needed. For example, they may be administered before going to the vet, an infrequent trip in the car, or prior to a thunderstorm. These medications tend to have a more dramatic effect on the dog's behaviour and tend to be used on an 'as needed' basis.

A key reason for the failure of a behaviour modification programme is non-compliance from the owner. Now, that's a pretty big over generalisation, and there are likely to be a number of reasons for the owner's non-compliance, including contributing factors from the behaviourist (see Chapter Three: The Human Factor In Canine Fear). However, I raise the issue again, within this chapter, because not all clients will be comfortable with a drug-based approach for their dog. If the owner has not had the opportunity to discuss their concerns, they may well be reluctant to go ahead with the treatment.

It is, therefore, important that the owner of a fearful dog is encouraged to make a list of queries and concerns before visiting the vet and ensure they get the answers they need to make an informed decision before commencing the course of treatment. Many of the drugs, which I am now going to discuss, need to be administered on a consistent schedule and may also need a period of 'weaning off' at the end of the treatment. This means it is essential to establish commitment and agreement to the approach before getting started.

THE HALF-LIFE

Prior to discussing specific drugs, we need to understand the 'half-life' concept. This relates to how long it takes for the drug in a dog's body to be reduced by half. This is affected by the way in which the body processes the drug, and then gets rid of it. The time span can vary from just a few hours through to a few days; however, no matter how long your dog has been taking the drug, the half-life is always the same.

It is important to be aware of a drug's half-life because medications with a longer half-life usually take longer to work, but can also mean fewer withdrawal symptoms. A drug with a short half-life may begin to show effects more quickly, but may also create more withdrawal problems. So, if a dog has been prescribed a drug with a short half-life and the decision is made to stop the medication, the vet may first consider switching to a related drug, with a longer half-life. This will, in turn, reduce the likelihood of the dog experiencing withdrawal side effects.

Abrupt discontinuation of medication can cause anxiety to reappear, so a gradual tapering off will be required. While it's important to consult your vet, a reduction of 25 per cent every one to two weeks is generally considered to be a safe guideline. This gradual discontinuation allows the owner to report any reappearance of the fearful behaviour and for guidance to be given on whether resuming the medication is recommended.

DAILY MEDICATIONS

This group of medications work by increasing the levels of particular neurotransmitters in the brain. For a more detailed explanation on the role of neurotransmitters, check out Chapter Two: The Physiological Basis Of Fear. But, essentially, these are the chemicals released as a result of specific stimulation and are used to transmit information from one neuron to the next; you could consider them having a messenger type role.

TRICYCLIC ANTI-DEPRESSANTS (TCAS)

These are an older form of drug, devised back in the 1950s, and were primarily prescribed as anti-depressants. The term tricyclic comes from their structure of three rings of atoms. Tricyclic anti-depressants work by preventing the reabsorption of the neurotransmitters, including serotonin and norepinephrine, so there will be more of them freely circulating in the synaptic cleft between the neurons in the brain. This change in both brain chemistry, and the communication within the brain nerve cell circuitry, is known to regulate mood.

Clomipramine is a TCA, which is licensed

for use in canine separation anxiety cases when administered alongside a behaviour modification plan. It has also proved to be helpful in some cases of storm phobias and more general anxiety disorders.

One of the issues with TCAs is that they are not very specific; they also have anti-inflammatory, analgesic, and sedative action, so that means that drowsiness is a common side effect. TCAs also come with a higher risk of toxicity with overdose, so maintaining a strict schedule of when medication is given, is very important. This medication is generally more effective when administered every 12 hours rather than every 24.

It can take three to four weeks to see the maximum effect of TCAs and a similar period of time to wean the dog off them at the end of treatment.

SELECTIVE SEROTONIN REUPTAKE INHIBITORS (SSRI)

Selective serotonin reuptake inhibitors increase the availability of serotonin. This is the neurotransmitter commonly associated with feelings of wellbeing and happiness. However, it does have quite a complex biological function, and also has a key function in cognition, reward, learning and memory.

SSRIs are specific for serotonin receptors so there can be the same benefits as with TCAs, but with fewer side effects, though there can be some drowsiness. Increased anxiety and, there has been some anecdotal reporting of increased aggression.

There is a much higher margin of safety in their use compared to TCAs with fewer risks associated with an overdose.

Commonly used SSRI drugs include fluoxetine (Reconcile® and Prozac®), paroxetine (Paxil®), sertraline (Zoloft®), and citalopram (Celexa®). These are prescribed to assist in the treatment of various anxieties and fears as well as compulsive disorders.

In most cases, it takes between two and four weeks to see the full effects, which are generally fairly subtle, but they do provide the opportunity to implement the behaviour modification plan. So this may mean that a dog taking an SSRI drug, doesn't become fearful as easily and, if the dog is triggered, his reactions may not be quite as intense. In addition, it becomes easier to distract, or redirect, the dog than previously.

SSRIs IN PRACTICE

To look at how a pharmacological option using a SSRI was implemented, let me introduce you to the case of Fizz, a Galgo/Podenco cross, who came to live with me, and my partner, David.

Background

Fizz had a tough start in life. Born on the streets of Madrid, he and his family evaded capture until six of the pups were eventually caught in a net. They were then taken on the five-hour drive down to the Galgos del Sol rescue centre in the Murcia region, which had kindly offered to take them in. It wasn't long, however, before all six pups became very unwell and parvovirus was diagnosed. Sadly, three of puppies didn't make it, but the remaining three youngsters returned to the rescue centre to recuperate. Unfortunately, Fizz was not yet finished with veterinary treatment as he developed a chest infection requiring another lengthy stay at the veterinary practice.

All of this happened during those critical periods when most pups would be out and about forming the positive associations which they would carry through into adulthood. For Fizz, his associations with people were based on the experience of being caught, and then the onslaught of the essential but intense medical treatment.

So Fizz came to stay with us as a foster to help him recuperate and to live in a home environment where the risk of further infection would be lower. Vaccinations had to be delayed due to his compromised immune system, and so any socialisation and habituation to the outside world had to be done very carefully.

While Fizz was an incredibly affectionate and loving dog with us, he was terrified of everybody else. Someone walking behind us was impossible for him to cope with and a visitor to the home caused a complete meltdown. Despite carefully organised visits from very understanding friends, Fizz remained unconvinced that he could trust anyone other than myself and David.

Further veterinary treatment was needed before Fizz was six months old, and when placed in the situation of needing to be in close contact with the vet, Fizz would completely shut down. He also urinated in fear, in one instance, all over the vet's footwear. See introduction.

A strong advantage of our home situation was that we lived in a very rural area, and so 'drop-in' visitors to the home were rare. Most visits by close friends or family were planned months in advance, which gave me the opportunity to brief them before they arrived. I described how Fizz might react and I also asked them not to encourage him to 'say hello' nor to interact with him should he come closer. Luckily our other dogs are very sociable, which provided visitors with a 'dog fix' should they want it.

Fizz coped with the visits, but an unexpected movement or appearance of a visitor would send him into a total state of panic.

The Psychopharmacological Plan

It quickly became clear that Fizz would need some form of psychopharmacological assistance to help him respond in a less fearful way, and to then be able to form new emotional responses towards unknown people.

The aim was not to sedate him, nor did we expect the medication to resolve all his problems. Instead, I was looking for a window of opportunity. I wanted Fizz to be in a state of mind where he could process information and form new points of reference for unknown people.

Fizz was prescribed fluoxetine at a dose of 20mg twice per day and we had a trial run before the first visitors arrived to check for any side effects. There was a slight sedative effect, but nothing that affected his day-to-day routine – he still loved to play with the other dogs and run around.

Put to the Test

When the visitors arrived, Fizz was still fearful and showing avoidance behaviour, but there was minimal barking. I was able to call him to me – something he had been unable to do previously. He did not want to eat a treat when they were offered to the other dogs, but he was curious as to what they were getting.

By the end of the six days, Fizz didn't react when someone came into the room; he was able to sleep when someone he didn't know was close by, and he had made tentative approaches towards them, to have a sniff. So great progress!

Moving Forward

Because of having few visitors to the home, other than a few holiday stays each summer, Fizz came off fluoxetine once we had the house to ourselves again. Under veterinary guidance, there was no requirement to taper off the medication as fluoxetine has a long half-life and Fizz had been taking it for less than eight weeks.

Over the following 18 months, this cycle was repeated and what we saw was an overall reduced level of anxiety, even when the medication was out of his system.

Fizz has now been with us for two and a half years and over the last year has not needed the fluoxetine, even when we have had visitors. We now live in a more urban environment, and he can continue to walk when someone is behind us, though he does like to take a quick look to check them out every now and then.

Finally, Fizz has other people in his life he trusts. Top of the list is our builder, Lee, who thankfully is a dog lover and doesn't mind Fizz's over-the-top adoration when he comes to do some work for us!

Summary

It is possible that, over a period of time, Fizz would have come to the same conclusion about strangers without the need for psychopharmacological intervention. However, this would have required many more instances of unknown people coming into his environment, along with all the risks of flooding taking place.

The fluoxetine provided Fizz with a break from the instant ignition of the sympathetic fight/flight system. This gave him the opportunity to assess situations and develop a new, positive history of interacting with people.

MONOAMINE OXIDASE INHIBITORS (MAOIS)

MAO is an enzyme that causes an increase in epinephrine, norepinephrine and serotonin. Anipryl (Selegiline) is an MAOI and has been found to be effective in treating chronic fears, phobias, and anxiety conditions. Typically it takes three to four weeks before an MAOI takes action.

MAOIs do have the potential for more significant side effects, and they can interact with other drugs, which enhance the serotonin system. These include some SSRI drugs, medication, such as tramadol, foods rich in tyramine, such as cheese, and nutraceuticals, such as turmeric and St. John's Wort.

This means that that the prescribing veterinarian must be aware of all medications the dog is taking – including herbal and parasiticides – before considering the suitability of MAOIs, to reduce the risk of serotonin syndrome, which can be fatal. The symptoms of serotonin syndrome include nausea, confusion, muscle rigidity and tremors, which could lead to seizures and coma.

SITUATIONAL MEDICATIONS

BENZODIAZEPINES

This class of medication works by enhancing the effects of GABA, an amino acid that operates as an inhibitory neurotransmitter in the brain. GABA's primary role is to reduce the activity of neurons in both the brain and the central nervous system. This results in the dog feeling more relaxed, with a reduction of stress and anxiety, and calmness of mood.

Pharmaceutical benzodiazepines include Alprazolam (Xanax), Diazepam (Valium) and Lorazepam (Ativan). For the maximum benefit, these medications need to be given at least an hour, and for some, at least two hours before the anxiety-producing stimuli is presented. This means careful watching of weather forecasts for storm phobias! Although the results of research are contradictory, there is some evidence that benzodiazepines are more likely to disinhibit aggression than other behavioural medications. This may be seen through bite inhibition being lessened. So, if there is any history of aggression, benzodiazepines are not generally recommended.

Other side effects include inhibiting learning, and amnesia. From this, you can see that they are unlikely to be a successful choice when used to supplement a behavioural medication plan. However for situational use, when behavioural approaches may be difficult to set-up and implement – such as fear caused by storms – they can be helpful in assisting a dog to cope.

TRAZADONE

Trazadone is a serotonin antagonist and reuptake inhibitor (SARI).This means that they act as antagonists to inhibit the 5HT2a serotonin receptor, and block the function of the serotonin transporter protein. As a result, they increase the amount of active serotonin throughout the central nervous system.

Trazodone is usually administered to minimise anxiety in short-term situations on an 'as needed' basis. It generally takes around two hours before relief is felt, although this can vary from dog to dog. Therefore, some testing may be required before using for a fear-inducing event, such as a visit to the vet.

Side effects can include a sedative effect, along with nausea and diarrhoea. It is not unusual for a combination of medications to be used to assist in fear cases; however, when trazadone is combined with an SSRI or TCA, there is a risk of serotonin syndrome. This occurs when brain levels of serotonin are too high. Symptoms include elevated heart rate and body temperature, tremors and shivering and difficulty breathing.

ALPHA-2 AGONISTS

The Alpha-2 receptors are found on cells within the sympathetic nervous system, which is the main 'excitatory' nervous system in the body. When alpha-2 receptors are stimulated, the sympathetic nervous system activity decreases and norepinephrine is blocked. In stressful situations, norepinephrine levels increase as part of the fight or flight response to get the body ready to react. This class of medication can, therefore, be helpful in situations where there is panic-driven response or intense reactivity.

Clonidine is an alpha-2 agonist administered in tablet form. It can take up to two hours to take effect and usually has a duration effect of around four to six hours. Another option is Sileo which is a transmucosal gel and is administered, via a syringe, to the dog's cheek and gums. It acts much more quickly – around 30 minutes – but lasts for a shorter period of time when compared to the tablets, generally around two hours.

Side effects of alpha-2 agonists have been reported to include dry mouth, sedation, and hypotension.

ACEPROMAZINE

Acepromazine or ACP, as it's often known, is a phenothiazine tranquilliser that has, historically, been used to decrease a dog's mobility and reactivity. While ACP slows down physical reactions, there is little effect on the anxiety that the dog will be experiencing; it may even worsen noise phobia in some dogs. For the fearful dog, this means being 'trapped' in a body that is not physically responding as it should, while feeling what may be increasing levels of fear.

This clearly means that ACP is not an appropriate medication for fear cases. However, it can be useful as an additional medication in situations where a dog is injuring himself as a result of his fearful response.

GABAPENTIN

Traditionally, Gabapentin has been utilised for the management of neuropathic pain and as an anticonvulsant. However, it is also used as an additional medication alongside an SSRI or TCA when these drugs used on their own, fail to significantly reduce anxiety levels.

Gabapentin binds to the alpha-2-delta subunit of presynaptic voltage sensitive calcium channels, and blocks the release of glutamate when there is excessive neurotransmission. It, therefore, reduces the release of excitatory neurotransmitters, which, in turn, decreases anxiety, aggression and avoidance behaviours.

Gabapentin generally requires one to two hours to take effect. Side effects are usually few and tend to be around gastrointestinal issues, i.e. loss of appetite, vomiting and diarrhoea.

NUTRACEUTICALS

Nutraceuticals are a range of natural products, or dietary supplements, which are marketed for the treatment of behavioural problems. They are available without the need for a prescription and can be used alone, or in combination, with prescribed medication. *For more information on nutraceuticals, see Chapter Eleven: Complementary Therapies.*

COMPLEMENTARY THERAPIES

In this chapter I will present a number of complementary therapies, which may be useful for the fearful dog, along with details of research into their efficacy, where it is available. If you are a behaviourist then it is important to check the legislation in your country to ensure that you understand what restrictions there may be with regard to making recommendations for complementary or alternative therapies, when assisting a client with a fearful dog.

I want to start this chapter with a definition of complementary therapy, as the term so often leads to misconceptions:

A complementary therapy is used alongside conventional behaviour modification approaches.

An alternative therapy is used in isolation.

Many behaviourists are supportive of clients using complementary therapies to assist the fearful dog. However, there are some who appear to be reluctant to agree to, or to promote their use. In most cases, this is because many therapies lack a history of scientific research. Fortunately this is changing and, slowly but surely, a trickle of research is emerging and is being published. This is significant, as it allows us to make a more informed decision on whether a complementary therapy may be a useful addition to a behavioural approach.

In many situations, the worst-case scenario of using a complementary therapy would be that there is no additional benefit. But there are exceptions and it's important not to fall into the trap of assuming that because a therapy is 'natural' then it can do no harm.

ACUPUNCTURE

The World Health Organisation lists acupuncture as a suitable treatment for anxiety and depression in humans; it is, therefore, not so surprising that it is considered to be a useful addition in programmes to assist fearful dogs. Although it is often seen as a complementary therapy, acupuncture is used in many UK medical practices, pain clinics and hospitals.

HOW IT WORKS
Derived from ancient Chinese medicine, acupuncture involves the insertion of fine needles at strategic points in the body.

Traditional Chinese medicine considers acupuncture as a technique for balancing the flow of energy or life force. This energy is known as chi or qi (chee), and it flows through pathways (meridians) in the body. The process of inserting needles into specific points along these meridians allows the energy flow to re-balance.

Western practitioners consider acupuncture within its context of being able to stimulate the sensory nerves under the skin and within the muscles. In turn, the body produces endorphins and oxytocin, which are pain and stress relieving chemicals. It is likely that these naturally released substances are responsible for the beneficial effects experienced with acupuncture. Neuro-imaging studies have confirmed that acupuncture can affect the autonomic nervous system which is the primary mechanism in control of the fight-or-flight response. More details on this system can be found in *Chapter Two: The Physiological Basis of Fear*.

RESEARCH

Kontogianis, K., Green, S. and Fanucchi, L. (2019). *'Acupuncture as a Modality for Treating Anxiety Related Disorders in Canines.'* Open Access Journal of Veterinary Science & Research, 4 (3).

The research process within this study included:

- Dogs from both shelter and home environments were included in the research
- Questionnaires completed by dog owners/guardians throughout the study.
- Heart rates taken before and after treatment.
- 6-10 weeks of treatment provided
- Observations to compare pre- and post-acupuncture behaviours.

When the researchers went on to consider the impact on the dogs' anxiety and aggression levels, there was a decline in the client-owned dogs, but the shelter dogs were reported to have very little to no improvement. The key limitation of this study comes from the very small sample size: just two dogs who lived in a home environment and two in a shelter took part.

Maccariello, C.E.M., Franzini de Souza, C.C., Morena, L., Dias, D.P.M. and Medeiros, M.A. (2018). *'Effects of acupuncture on the heart rate variability, cortisol levels and behavioural response induced by thunder sound in Beagles.'* Physiology and Behavior, 186, pp.37-44.

This laboratory study aimed to evaluate the effects of acupuncture on a number of different factors including reactive responses after being exposed to the sound of thunder.

A total of 24 dogs with no history of phobia to thunder were split into three groups: those who would receive acupuncture, those who had needles inserted in non-acupuncture points and a control group who had no needles inserted. Twenty minutes later, a recording of thunder, over a 150 second period with a maximum intensity of 103-104 dB, was played to each group of dogs.

Comparing the results between the groups, the researchers found that the dogs who did receive acupuncture showed reduced rates of hiding, restlessness, bolting and running around behaviours.

SIDE EFFECTS AND RISKS

Acupuncture is considered to be a very safe form of treatment when administered by a veterinarian who is fully trained in the procedure. It is rare to see side effects, but they do occur. Conditions can seem worse for up to 48 hours after treatment, and sometimes animals appear lethargic or sleepy for 24 hours. It is considered that these effects are an indication of the development of physiological changes and that they will be followed by improvement in the animal's condition.

AROMATHERAPY

Aromatherapy is a holistic, healing treatment that utilises natural plant extracts to promote health and wellbeing. The essential oils used within aromatherapy are made from essences found in a plant's seeds, blossoms, fruit, leaves, stems, or roots. Although the term 'aromatherapy' did not appear until the 1900s, the concept has been around for thousands of years.

HOW IT WORKS

Lemon oil, for example, has been found to improve moods, even though there doesn't appear to be a significant physiological response to the oil, such as a reduction in heart rate or blood pressure. However it has been found that the mitral cells, which carry the information about a scent to your brain, and allows you to recognise a smell, also carry the information to other parts of the brain including the amygdala. This structure in the brain is involved in emotional learning and memory, which explains why smells are often linked to specific memories.

When thinking about aromatherapy and the fearful dog, the use of lavender oil has been suggested as having a positive effect on the dog's responses. Critics have, however, claimed that this may be due to the scent of the oil distracting the dog from whatever is causing the fear rather than the oil changing his response. It is also suggested that, before using an essential oil, it should be paired with a positive emotion, which would develop the link between a smell and positive memory. This might mean, for example, presenting the oil and then giving the dog a treat. In time the smell becomes a predictor of good things happening.

RESEARCH

Graham, L., Wells, D.L. and Hepper, P.G. (2005). *'The influence of olfactory stimulation on the behaviour of dogs housed in a rescue shelter.'* Applied Animal Behavior Science 91 (1-2) pp.143-153.

This study looked at the effect of four different odours – lavender, chamomile, rosemary and peppermint – on the behaviour of 55 dogs in a rescue shelter. The dogs were exposed to each odour, via a diffuser, for four hours each day over a five-day period. There was then a period of two days when the dogs were not exposed to an odour before the next one was trialled. During each five-day period, the researchers recorded the dogs' behaviour on days one, three and five.

During the periods when the dogs were exposed to lavender and chamomile, they spent more time resting, and less time moving, compared to the periods when they were exposed to other odours, and to no odour in the control period. They also found that there was less vocalisation. However, the diffusion of rosemary and peppermint encouraged much more standing, moving and vocalising.

SIDE EFFECTS AND RISKS
Essential oils are potent substances that can pose serious risks when misused; a few drops can make a significant difference to that risk level. Oils used incorrectly can lead to changes in behaviour, adverse effects on the central nervous system, and respiratory problems. It is, therefore, highly recommended that you seek professional advice, or use one of the pre-formulated products which incorporate dog-safe essential oils.

BACH FLOWER REMEDIES

It was Edward Bach, a British homeopath and physician, who developed the range of Bach Flower Remedies (BRF). Bach experimented with the highly diluted derivatives of 37 different species of wildflowers which were obtained by boiling the flowers, leaves, and twigs in natural spring water, or by placing the flower heads and spring water in direct sunlight. Bach practitioners believe that the water captures the 'essence' of the flower and 'potentises' its healing power. The resulting plant-water mixture, combined with an alcohol-based preservative, is called the 'mother tincture'. The final, diluted over-the counter products labelled 'flower essences' and 'flower remedies' can be administered orally in drop form, as skin compresses and as whole-body baths.

HOW IT WORKS
Bach practitioners believe that the remedies exert a positive effect on the human energy field, resulting in their

ability to correct emotional imbalances. BFRs are taken both for specific short-term emotional stresses, such as during the firework season, as well as for managing or controlling long-term emotional problems.

BFRs can be used individually or in combination with Rescue Remedy (RR) which is one of the best-known combinations. RR consists of five flower essences: cherry plum (*Prunus cerasifera*), clematis (*Clematis vitalba*), impatiens (*Impatiens glandulifera*), Star of Bethlehem (*Ornithogalum umbellatum*), and rock rose (*Helianthemum nummularium*). When combined, they are believed to act together to reduce or eliminate stress.

RESEARCH

This is where we come to a halt because, as far as I can see, there has been no published research on the use of Bach Flower Remedies and their use in canine fear. There has been limited research into the use of Rescue Remedy and human anxiety, but this concluded that it was of no greater effect than the placebo.

So, perhaps, a little leap of faith is needed to consider their use. BFRs are essentially gentle and non-toxic. Assuming they are not used inappropriately, there is anecdotal evidence that they can be helpful when used alongside a behaviour modification plan.

SIDE EFFECTS AND RISKS

BFRs are described as non-toxic, and Bach specialists state that there are no side effects resulting from their use. Practitioners report that the use of BFRs do not interact with other medications which may be taken at the same time. There have been no clinical trials to demonstrate their safety, although Bach practitioners state there have been no reports of serious adverse effects in their records, which go back to 1970.

CANNABIS EXTRACT, CBD

Cannabis has been used as a medicinal remedy for centuries for the treatment of numerous ailments, including anxiety and depression. Cannabis (often referred to as marijuana) and hemp are two varieties of the same plant species, Cannabis sativa.

Cannabis has higher levels of THC, which is the psychoactive cannabinoid responsible for the 'high' experienced with cannabis use. The hemp plant, meanwhile, has less than 0.3 per cent THC and 12-18 per cent cannabidiol (CBD). CBD is the non-psychoactive molecule, which is increasingly being suggested as an effective treatment in humans for conditions ranging from chronic pain to anxiety and insomnia. Not surprisingly, interest in the use of CBD for pets has also grown.

HOW IT WORKS

The hypothalamus is a specialised region of the brain; it has a series of receptors on its surface that scan the blood for cortisol levels. When there is an influx of cortisol in the blood, these receptors respond by feeding back to the adrenal glands to stop production of stress hormones. However, if a dog becomes chronically stressed, the hypothalamus becomes less sensitive to cortisol, meaning it will need more cortisol to get the same response. This, in turn, means that the dog will remain stressed for long periods of time

CBD is said to boost the ability of the hypothalamus to sense cortisol. This then triggers the shut-off valve much sooner and prevents stress from lingering for too long.

A second suggested function of CBD relates to its stimulation of the neuro-transmitter, GABA. GABA acts as the brake pedal in the brain; it tells it to slow down and relax. It is one of the primary neuro-transmitters involved with the 'rest and digest' nervous system, and it holds the key to turning down the stress response.

Many anti-anxiety medications work by boosting GABA activity in the brain which, essentially, allows us to slow down and relax.

RESEARCH

Jurkus, R., Day, H.L., Guimarães, F.S., Lee, J.L.C., Bertoglio, L.J. and Stevenson, C.W. (2016) *'Cannabidiol Regulation of Learned Fear: Implications for Treating Anxiety-Related Disorders.'* Frontiers in Pharmacology 7 (454).

There is a growing number of articles being published on the use of CBD to help people with anxiety problems. However, at the time of writing, there are no studies which focus on its effectiveness in assisting fearful dogs. This research was carried out in a laboratory with the aim of understanding the value of CBD for humans suffering from anxiety and trauma-related disorders, such as phobias and PTSD. However, its findings could also provide helpful information into whether CBD may offer a valuable addition to the behaviour modification of fearful dogs.

Researchers in this study assessed the effect of CBD on a learnt fear, in this case where rats had learnt that a particular auditory tone would result in receiving a shock. So when the rats heard the tone, even without a shock being applied, they became fearful. While the cannabidiol did not reduce fear when receiving a shock, the researchers found that when they began the extinction process of playing the tone, but not applying a shock, the rats that had been given cannabidiol expressed less fear.

To place this in a canine context, imagine a dog becoming fearful of getting into a car following an incident where he had been traveling in a car and had been involved in an accident. The results from this research suggest that CBD would reduce the fear the dog would feel when travelling in a car, but it would not prevent fear if there was another accident.

The researchers summarised their findings by stating that there was evidence to indicate that cannabidiol reduces learned fear in three different ways:

1. It decreases the expression of fear.
2. It disrupts memory reconsolidation, leading to the reduction of fear upon memory retrieval.
3. It enhances extinction; a process by which learned fear is reduced.

Many of the fears that our dogs develop are the result of a learning experience rather than being instinctual responses. This may mean that, following further research, CBD may prove to be a useful addition to the behaviourist's toolbox.

SIDE EFFECTS AND RISKS
Many of the potential issues around the use of CBD come from ensuring the quality of the product and that it is THC free. Dogs have many more cannabinoid receptors in their brain, and throughout their body, so this means that THC can be overwhelming and that poisoning from CBD can be fatal.

Another consideration is the potential for drug interactions. Most prescription medications are metabolised in the liver by way of specific enzymes produced in the organ. The cytochrome P450 enzyme is critical in metabolising as much as 60 per cent of medication; however, CBD may temporarily inhibit its availability. It is, therefore, essential to advise your vet if CBD has been given to your dog when other medications are being considered.

PRESSURE WRAPS

A pressure wrap provides a constant and steady pressure across the dog's chest while still allowing him to move around. Several commercial products are now available, including the Thundershirt® and The Original Anxiety Wrap®.

HOW IT WORKS
Theoretically, the wraps apply pressure to the dog's torso which causes a calming effect similar to swaddling a crying infant or hugging a distressed person.

When you hug someone, pressure receptors under the skin are stimulated. As a result, there is an increase in activity within the parasympathetic system, through the vagal nerves. It is the stimulation of these nerves that triggers an increase in oxytocin levels. Often called 'the bonding hormone' because it promotes attachment in relationships, oxytocin is made primarily in the hypothalamus in the brain. While some of it is released into the bloodstream through the pituitary gland, some remains in the brain, where it influences mood, behaviour and physiology. The act of hugging, and the oxytocin release which comes with it, can have trickle-down effects throughout the body, causing a decrease in heart rate and a drop in the stress hormones, cortisol and norepinephrine.

Another theory on how pressure wraps may work is from the perspective of acupressure. Based on the same principles as acupuncture, acupressure aims to free blocked, or out of balance meridians which run through the body. This, in turn, allows the vital energy or life force called qi (ch'i) to flow freely. So, it has been suggested that the close fitting wraps act on acupressure points to restore balance.

RESEARCH

Cottam, N., Dodman, N.H. and Ha, J.C. (2013). 'The effectiveness of the Anxiety Wrap in the treatment of canine thunderstorm phobia: An open-label trial.' Journal of Veterinary Behavior, 8, pp.154-161.

This research looked at how the Anxiety Wrap may help dogs with thunderstorm phobia. They compared the owner's assessment of their dog's thunderstorm anxiety before and after the use of the wrap. After five uses of the Anxiety Wrap, 89 per cent of owners reported that it was at least partially effective in treating their dogs' thunderstorm anxiety.

The researchers did highlight that the decrease in anxiety scores could be due to a placebo effect. Owners had been informed that the product could have a positive impact on their dogs' thunderstorm anxiety. Therefore owners' expectations may have influenced their perceptions of how well the wrap worked. The researchers also considered that providing the owners with a plan of action to address their dogs' fears could have changed their body language in a way that caused the dogs to feel more secure.

King, C.,Buffington, L., Smith, T.J. and Grandin, T. (2014). 'The effect of a pressure wrap (ThunderShirt®) on heart rate and behaviour in canines diagnosed with anxiety disorder.' Journal of Veterinary Behavior 9, (5)pp. 215-221.

This study investigated the use of a pressure wrap (ThunderShirt) on heart rate and behaviour in dogs who had previously been diagnosed with anxiety disorder. A total of 90 dogs took part, and they were randomly assigned to one of three groups:

Group 1: The dogs wore the ThunderShirt per manufacturer's recommendations.

Group 2: The dogs wore the ThunderShirt loosely, without pressure.

Group 3: The control group where the dogs had no specific treatment.

The researchers measured each dog's average and maximum heart rate at the start of the experiment, and then again after 15 minutes alone in the kennel. The researchers' video-recorded the dogs and then analysed the recordings looking for the presence of 12 different behaviours. These included pacing, panting, yawning and howling.

Results from this study showed that dogs that wore the ThunderShirt to the manufacturer's specifications had lowered heart rate, decreased visual orientation towards the door (looking for their owner), as well as reduced yawning and tongue-flicking stress compared to Group 2 and Group 3, the control group.

SIDE EFFECTS AND RISKS

Some owners report that their dogs seem to become 'stuck' when a pressure wrap is applied. This freezing behaviour is likely to be the response to the unusual feeling of the 'hug' sensation. For these dogs it's important to introduce the wrap slowly and well in advance of the time when it is needed. This allows you to increase the pressure gradually until it meets the manufacturer's guidelines.

HOMEOPATHY

Homeopathy is a holistic medicine which uses highly diluted substances with the aim of triggering the body's own healing mechanisms. Though homeopathy dates back to Hippocrates (460-377BC), it has been used in its current form, across the world, for some 200 years. The word homeopathy is derived from the Greek words homeo, meaning 'similar,' and pathos, meaning 'suffering.'

HOW IT WORKS

Homeopathy is based on the principle of 'like treats like.' This means that a substance, which causes symptoms when taken in large doses, can be used in small amounts to treat similar symptoms by triggering the body's natural defences. Homoeopaths are of the view that the lower the dosage, the more effective a treatment can be.

The nano-particles within the remedies are believed to have properties which provide them with greater bioavailability. This is a measure of how easily a substance can be absorbed by the body. In the context of pharmacology, it refers to how quickly a drug enters the circulatory system and reaches the desired area, so that it can then take effect. They also initiate a process called hormesis, which refers to the way the body adapts, over time, to low levels of stressors or toxins. When faced with an infectious agent, or cumulative stress, the body can change from a healthy to an unhealthy state.

Homeopathic remedies are said to work by hormetically signalling the organism to reverse the many adaptations it has made to combat infection or chronic stressors. This, therefore, means that the remedies trigger the body's innate ability to heal.

To produce homeopathic medicine, the ingredients are weakened through the addition of water or alcohol. The mixture is then shaken in a process called 'potentisation' which homoeopaths believe is required to transfer the healing essence.

RESEARCH

Cracknell, N. and Mills, D. (2008). *'A double-blind placebo-controlled study into the efficacy of a Homeopathic remedy for fear of firework noises in the dog (Canis familiaris)'.* The Veterinary Journal 177 pp.80-88.

This research involved a study group of 75 dogs that showed a fear response to fireworks. The dogs were assigned to a homeopathic treatment or to a placebo treatment, which was a preparation of water and 20 per cent alcohol. The homeopathic treatment was (verum), based on phosphorus, rhododendron, borax, theridion,and chamomilla. The owners were then asked to identify the behavioural signs of fear that their

dogs usually displayed in response to fireworks along with rating their frequency and intensity.

After four weeks of using either the homeopathic treatment or the placebo, owners were asked to rate the frequency and intensity of each behaviour that their dogs displayed to fireworks during the treatment period.

Interestingly, the placebo group reported that there were significant improvements in 14/15 behavioural signs of fear from their dogs. The homeopathic group stated there was an improvement in all 15 of the behavioural signs.

SIDE EFFECTS AND RISKS

Homeopathic remedies are generally safe, and the risk of a severe adverse side effect arising from taking these remedies is thought to be small. Some homeopathic remedies may contain substances that are not safe or interfere with the action of other medicines.

When considering homeopathy as a complementary approach to a behaviour modification plan, it is recommended that you enlist the assistance of a homeopathic vet who can guide the treatment.

HOMEOPATHY VERSUS BACH FLOWER REMEDIES

Homeopathy and Bach Flower Remedies do have similarities in that they both use the principle of dilution. Homoeopaths tend to use a stronger dilution than that which is used for Bach Flower Remedies, and the process of dilution also differs. In addition, Bach Flower therapy doesn't potentise, i.e. it doesn't involve shaking the bottle between every potency.

Bach Flower therapy only uses flowers from non-harmful plants, shrubs and trees, whereas homeopathy uses plants, minerals and animal substances. Some homeopathic medicines can have a strong effect and so cannot be given without advice to at risk groups. This means that great care needs to be taken if they are prescribed for dogs. In contrast, Bach Flower therapy can be given without any risk; they are entirely harmless even in high dosage.

Homeopathy is based on the philosophy that the body, mind and emotions are not separate and distinct, but instead are fully integrated. Based on this perspective, a homeopath seeks a remedy that fits all of a patient's physical and psychological symptoms. Bach Flower therapy only focuses on the emotional and mental wellbeing of the person.

NUTRACEUTICALS

Nutraceutical is a broad term used to describe any product derived from food sources which have extra health benefits in addition to their basic nutritional value. The term 'nutraceutical', which has no legal definition, combines two words, nutrient (a nourishing food component) and pharmaceutical (a medical drug). Within the animal world, these products may be described as an animal dietary supplement rather than a nutraceutical.

Nutraceuticals which may be helpful to the fearful dog, include the following:

1. Zylkene®

Zylkene® is promoted as being able to enhance relaxed behaviour in pets. It contains alpha-casozepine, an ingredient derived from a milk protein which has calming properties. It binds to the GABAA receptors in the brain and mimics the action of GABA, an inhibitory neuro-transmitter. This mechanism of action is similar to that of benzodiazepines, which are known to reduce anxiety. However, alpha-casozepine does not create the sedative-like side effects associated with benzodiazepines.

RESEARCH

Beata, C., Beaumont-Graff, E., Diaz, C., Marion, M. Massal, N. Marlois, N., Muller, G. and Lefranc, C. (2007). *'Effects of alpha-casozepine (Zylkene) versus selegiline hydrochloride (Selgian, Anipryl) on anxiety disorders in dogs.'* Journal of Veterinary Behavior 2, pp.175–183.

In this study, a total of 38 dogs were recruited within veterinary practices by certified behaviourist surgeons to take part in a 56-day trial. Each dog had been diagnosed as having an anxiety related behaviour problem and scored 19, or above, on a scale designed to evaluate emotional disorders in dogs. In addition to the medication, owners were also asked to follow a specially designed behaviour modification plan

The results showed that, while not all dogs responded to the treatments provided, selegiline and alpha-casozepine (Zylkene) were shown to be equally effective.

2. L-theanine

L-theanine is an amino acid commonly found in green tea and mushrooms. Claimants believe it has the ability to decrease signs of anxiety by increasing dopamine, serotonin, and gamma-aminobutyric acid (GABA) levels.

Anxitane® is a purified L-theanine product which comes in the form of a chewable tablet. It is marketed to help pets keep calm and relaxed, and its recommended use is in conjunction with a behaviour modification plan. Its effectiveness has been tested in both clinical and laboratory studies.

RESEARCH

Araujoa, J.A., de Riveraa,C., Ethierb, J.L., Landsberg, G.M., Denenberg, S. Arnold, S. and Milgrama, N.W. (2010). *'ANXITANE (R) tablets reduce fear of human beings in a Laboratory model of anxiety-related behaviour'.* Journal of Veterinary Behavior Clinical Applications and Research 5(5) pp.268-275.

The researchers in this study found that when dogs who were already fearful of unknown people were given ANXITANE® tablets, they showed greater human interaction and approach than the control group and showed no side effects. They concluded that ANXITANE® tablets are effective for reducing fearful behaviour in dogs towards unfamiliar people.

A limitation of this study comes from the number of dogs who were assessed, with there being just five dogs in the control group and five receiving the ANXITANE® tablets.

Pike, A.L., Horwitz, D,F. and Loprise, H. (2015). *'An open-label prospective study of the use of l-theanine (Anxitane) in storm-sensitive client-owned dogs'.* Journal of Veterinary Behavior 10 (4) pp. 324-331.

This study suggests that l-theanine can be an effective treatment for storm sensitivity. Owners were asked to assess their dogs after an initial storm and then again after each of five subsequent storms. A total of 18 dogs took part in the study and all were given the manufacturer's recommended dosage of ANXITANE®.

The researchers found that there was treatment success in achieving an overall decrease in the severity of the dogs' responses to the storm, along with the time it took for them to return to baseline once the storm had ended. Reductions in the number of fear responses including drooling, following people, pacing, panting, and hiding were also reported.

3. Harmonease

Harmonease is a blend of a patented extract of Magnolia officinalis and a proprietary extract of Phellodendron amurense. These compounds have been reported to decrease mild, transient stress and the derivatives, honokiol and magnolol from Magnolia, have been shown to have in vitro GABAA modulation capability.

RESEARCH

DePorter, D.L., Landsberg, D.M., Araujo, J.A., Ethier, J.L. and Bledsoe, D, L. (2012). *'Harmonease Chewable Tablets reduces noise-induced fear and anxiety in a laboratory canine thunderstorm situation: a blinded and placebo-controlled study.'* J Vet Behav: Clin Appl Res. 7 pp. 225–232.

Thunderstorm simulation was used as a means of inducing fearful and anxious behaviour, which was evidenced through increased inactivity or freezing. A total of 20 dogs were included in this study, with half receiving Harmonease, and half a placebo, for a period of seven days. After a seven-day period without treatment or placebo, the groups were swapped so that after 21 days, all dogs had been in both the Harmonease and placebo groups. To assess the effectiveness of Harmonease, thunderstorm noise was played through a speaker system, and the dog's response was measured.

Researchers found that 12 of 20 (60 per cent) dogs improved when treated with Harmonease, whereas only 5 of 20 (25 per cent) improved on placebo. Additionally, 9 of 20 (45 per cent) placebo dogs showed increased inactivity duration, so their response worsened, whereas only 4 of 20 (20 per cent) treated dogs showed a worse response.

PHEROMONETHERAPY

In 1959, Peter Karlson, a German biochemist and and Martin Lüscher, a Swiss entomologist, proposed the term 'pheromones' as being the "substances secreted to the outside by an individual and received by a second individual of the same species, in which they release a specific reaction, for example, a definite behaviour or developmental process".

Pheromones, also described as semio-chemicals, are chemical cocktails which are designed to affect behaviour. In dogs, pheromone-producing areas include the anal sacs, ears, footpads and genitalia.

HOW IT WORKS

Pheremontherapy is the use of chemical signals, typically used in communication between animals of the same species, but it can also be used to allow humans to manage the behaviour of animals.

Adaptil® is a synthetic version of the dog appeasing pheromone which is released from the mammary glands of the mother dog, and promotes calm behaviour in her young. Adaptil® is available as a spray, a diffuser or an impregnated collar. It is recommended for separation-related problems, sound sensitivity, and general anxiety related problems such as being in new places or meeting new people.

RESEARCH

Landsberg, G. M., Beck, A., Lopez, A., Deniaud, M., Araujo, J.A. and Milgram, N.W. (2015). *'Dog-appeasing pheromone collars reduce sound-induced fear and anxiety in Beagle dogs: a placebo-controlled study.'* Veterinary Record 177: 260.

The objective of this study was to assess the effects of a dog-appeasing pheromone (DAP) collar in reducing sound-induced fear and anxiety in a thunderstorm simulation.

A total of 24 Beagles were divided into two treatment groups (DAP and placebo). Each group was then exposed to thunderstorm simulation tests, and the dogs' responses were assessed on a six-point scale for active (increased activity) and passive (decreased activity) fear. The dogs were also given a global score which took into account all signs of fear, both active and passive.

DAP was found to significantly decrease global fear and anxiety both during and post thunder simulation when compared with baseline measurements. There was no significant improvement in the placebo group from baseline on the test days.

What does need to be taken into account was that this research was undertaken within a clinical setting, and so was without many of the triggers which might cause thunderstorm fear and anxiety. These can include changes in the wind and barometric pressure, darkening skies and lightning. It's also important to consider how the owner's responses can influence the development and progression of the problem.

Osella, C.M., Bergamasco, L., Odore, L., Beck, A. and Gazzano, A. (2015) *'Adaptive mechanisms in dogs adopted from shelters: a behavioural assessment of the use of a synthetic analogue of the canine appeasing pheromone.'* Dog Behavior 2, pp.1-12.

Moving to a new home can be a difficult transition for dogs who have been adopted from a rescue environment. When dogs struggle to cope with unfamiliar surroundings, it can reduce the likelihood of successful rehoming. The aim of this study was to investigate the effects of Adaptil® in dogs rehomed from rescue shelters. This involved providing the new owners of 32 dogs with an Adaptil® diffuser. Owners were visited twice, at approximately four weeks and seven weeks, and asked to complete a questionnaire about their new dog's behaviour. This included the dog's ability to settle, their reaction to unfamiliar people and how they coped when left alone.

The researchers found that there were significant decreases in the number of behaviours by the time the owners completed the second questionnaire. This included a significant decrease in the dogs' reactions to being left alone and hiding fearfully in protected corners of the home. The researchers concluded that DAP might improve dogs' adaptability during the first weeks following adoption and could be considered a useful tool for reducing stress in rehomed dogs.

However, there are limitations with this study, most particularly that there was no comparison control group, and that there was no baseline measurement taken of the dogs' behaviour prior to the use of DAP.

SIDE EFFECTS AND RISKS

There are no known long-term side effects of the DAP collar. Obviously, care is needed to ensure that a dog has no open wound in the neck area when using a DAP collar to reduce the likelihood of any irritation. From a human perspective, the manufacturers of the plug-in ADAPTIL® diffuser recommend that it is not used in a non-ventilated room where people spend most of their time, and also that it is not to be used in bedrooms.

TTOUCH

Developed by Linda Tellington-Jones, Tellington Ttouch is described as "a gentle, respectful method of training, that honours the body, mind and spirit of animals and their people and develops trust between humans and animals".

Along with the equipment used, such as body wraps, there are two key aspects to the approach:

1. **Body work:** This is called Tellington TTouch. It utilises circular TTouches which are believed to reduce fear and pain. It is also claimed that it can enhance cellular function and communication and support the healing potential of the body. A number of different Ttouches are utilised for different effect. With the 'Tarantulas pulling the plow', for example, the practitioner walks their

fingers gently up the dog's back, like a spider, while letting the thumbs drag behind, like a plough. This touch is said to help stimulate circulation and may be helpful for dogs with touch sensitivity.

While body work may sound similar to massage, there is a key difference. In TTouch, the skin is moved lightly in one and a quarter circles using the tips of the fingers. The aim is to simply move the skin, rather than pressing down into underlying tissues, a prerequisite of massage.

When touch is used in a way which the dog finds pleasurable, there is the potential for the stimulation of oxytocin production. This, in turn, may elevate mood and slow the heart. Using the methods and techniques promoted within Ttouch ensures that the dog finds it a pleasurable experience while also teaching the owner how to observe and respond to their dog's responses.

2. **Ground work:** This is called the 'Playground for higher learning'. Tension affects both movement and balance and, as a result, both confidence and coping ability can be affected. There are many factors that affect physical balance, from a young puppy learning to co-ordinate his growing body through to an older dog coping with age related skeletal issues. Ground work exercises use objects on the ground to encourage the dog to slow his pace and become more aware of his movement.

RESEARCH

Lloyd, J. and Roe, E. (2013) *Using TTouch to Reduce Stress and Enhance Learning when Training Guide Dogs.* International Journal of Orientation & Mobility 6, (1).

At present, there are no studies which focus on the effectiveness of Ttouch and fearful dogs. However, this article discusses a range of studies and literature, across a number of species, along with the benefits that touch, in a more general sense, can bring.

SIDE EFFECTS AND RISKS

It is strongly recommended that you attend a short course, before using TTouch, in order to fully understand the techniques and their application. This will also help you to monitor your dog when using Ttouch and ensure that he finds it a positive experience. Alternatively, you may find the best approach is to refer to, or contact, an experienced TTouch practitioner.

In this chapter I discuss techniques that I would not recommend for assisting a dog to overcome his fears. I have detailed reasons for these decisions along with the risks associated with their use.

If only dogs came with manuals, then it would be easy to know what to do in any given situation! But just as with many problems in life, there is more than one way to approach helping a fearful dog and that, in itself, creates its own challenges.

A quick search of Google for help with a fearful dog brings nearly 20 million suggested pages. While some will provide helpful advice, there will also be those which may make the problem worse and may be hugely detrimental to the relationship you have with your dog.

To help you find a way through this maze, I am focusing on two of the best known 'don't go there' techniques – positive punishment and flooding. Both of these are widely promoted on the television, the internet and in other publications, as methods to help the fearful dog. I should add that each of these *may* resolve, or *appear* to resolve, the problem but the risks of things going wrong are immense.

POSITIVE PUNISHMENT

Punishment results in a decrease in the strength of a behaviour due to its consequences. So if there is a consequence, which we, or our dogs, find sufficiently unpleasant, we may stop performing the associated behaviour. Although this sounds very straightforward, there is a host of issues associated with this approach to modifying behaviour.

Positive punishment requires the addition (hence the positive) of something that is so aversive, that the likelihood of the dog repeating the behaviour is greatly reduced. This could be an e-collar, the jerk of a lead, a verbal reprimand – anything that is an addition to the situation with the intent of stopping a behaviour.

For clarity, when punishment is discussed within this section of the book, I am referring to positive punishment. You may also see reference to negative punishment when searching for resources to help your fearful dog. This involves the removal (hence the term 'negative') of something which the dog finds desirable in order to reduce the likelihood of the behaviour happening again. So, removing the opportunity to get a treat if your dog stands, rather than sits when asked, would be negative punishment.

BUT CAN WE PUNISH AN EMOTION?

Fearful dogs may show a range of physical responses when feeling worried. These are being driven by the environment, in which they find themselves, in just the same way as behavioural responses are occurring. While we could punish the dog for these physical reactions, the environment is still causing the fearful emotions to take place.

These physical signals are hugely beneficial in helping us to identify a dog's feelings of anxiety or fear. Without this evidence, we might struggle to understand when a dog needs help, and when he may need to be removed from a situation that is causing him concern. When a dog has been punished in this situation, he may stop showing the outward signs of fear, despite feeling the emotion. Now the dog has lost a key way to communicate with us. As a result, we may only become aware of an issue when the dog has become so overwhelmed that he perceives his only available option is to take top-level action, which may mean a snap or a bite.

When a fearful dog is in a situation that worries him, he already feels stress and lacks confidence, so punishment for showing fear is highly unlikely to improve matters. Additionally, the stress response is likely to inhibit new learning from even taking place.

It's the cerebrum area of the brain that is of key interest when we are considering behavioural problems in pets. The cerebral cortex is involved in problem solving and logical thought processes, so it is of crucial importance when a dog needs to learn a new behaviour. In addition, the cerebrum is the emotional centre of the brain, which is known as the limbic system.

When a dog becomes aroused, the limbic system – the emotional brain – kicks in. When this happens, it overrides the cortical system – the thinking and logical part of the brain. Therefore when a dog is experiencing fear, his ability to listen or learn is severely compromised. Suddenly all those behaviours, which the dog could perform perfectly well at home seem to have disappeared. Now that doesn't mean we cannot successfully transfer learnt behaviours to situations that cause fear. It just means we need to utilise them as part of a gradual and structured approach. For more information see *Chapter Two: The Physiological Basis of Fear*.

If we take into account that a dog may abandon physical signalling when he is punished, and that fear may override his ability to process information and learn, we can quickly come to the conclusion that the use of punishment to reduce fearful behaviour is likely to be both ineffective and unethical. However, if any further evidence is needed as to why this is an inappropriate approach, let us delve a little deeper into the issues relating to the use of punishment.

WHAT IS PUNISHING?

We all have different interpretations both as to what we find punishing, and what we find not punishing. We also need to be aware that those definitions can change depending on the circumstances we find ourselves in. If, for example, you are struggling financially, receiving a speeding fine may be very punishing and you will be likely to pay meticulous attention to the speed limit thereafter. If, however, you have large amounts of disposable income, the fine may have little effect on your behaviour other than being a mild annoyance.

This is just the same for our dogs. A playful smack on the rear for many Labradors results in a wag of the tail and the start of a game. For a more sensitive breed, it may have a devastating consequence. Only your dog can decide if your action is punishing or not, and that will become evident by whether there is a reduction in the undesirable behaviour.

PUNISHMENT MAY RESULT IN AN AGGRESSIVE RESPONSE

Imagine you are working with a dog who has fear issues; the very last thing you want to encourage in that situation is an aggressive response. But

that is just what researchers from the School of Veterinary Medicine at the University of Pennsylvania found was a frequent consequence of using positive punishment.

The severity of the aggressive response depended on the severity of the technique used to punish the dog. A total of 43 per cent of the dogs increased their aggression in response to physical punishment, such as being hit or kicked, while 3 per cent showed an increase in aggression in response to a corrective sound, such as "schhtt!" or "uh-uh!".

We may be under the impression that we understand our dogs, and we know what response we would be likely to get if we were to use punishment. However, because we believe that we can 'get away with it' with an aggressive response occurring, it doesn't make it any more of an ethical approach to take.

Herron, M.E., Shofer, F.S. and Reisner, I.R. (2009). 'Survey of the use and outcome of confrontational and non-confrontational training methods in client-owned dogs showing undesired behaviors'. *Applied Animal Behavior Science* 117 pp. 47-54

PUNISHMENT ONLY TEACHES WHAT NOT TO DO

Remember that definition of positive punishment: its intent is to reduce the likelihood of a behaviour. So now our fearful dog has learnt not to show the physical signs of being worried, what should he do instead? He is still feeling the emotion of fear even if he is suppressing his body language. The result we often see is a dog who becomes shut down. To the untrained eye, it can look as if the dog is calm, but if we really observe that dog, we can see that he is unresponsive, he may avoid eye contact, and he is guarded in his body language.

With our fearful dogs, we need to focus on providing them with the opportunity to learn new emotional responses to situations which previously caused fear.

IT'S DETRIMENTAL TO THE RELATIONSHIP BETWEEN DOG AND OWNER

Fearful dogs quickly learn what constitutes a threat. In fact, the fear may have developed after a single, frightening experience. If we think about this from an evolutionary perspective, it makes perfect sense. If you escaped from a lion the first time, then you are going to learn from that one experience and keep out of its way next time.

That is precisely what can happen if a dog has a frightening experience with a person. Rather than being a predictable source of reassurance and safety, people, in general, become an unpredictable force in the dog's life and need to be avoided. The punished dog has learnt that he needs to avoid the source of the fear, the owner. Not only does our fearful dog still have that original fear, he now has a new one to contend with as well.

THE DEGREE OF PUNISHMENT USED TENDS TO ESCALATE

When punishment is used, it tends to suppress a behaviour. It reduces the likelihood of the behaviour being demonstrated rather than eradicating it. However, how do you know the 'correct' level of punishment intensity to use? As I have already mentioned, we don't really know what that right level is until it has been applied, and the results are assessed. We also have to consider that the owner will have an emotional bond to the dog. It is, therefore, likely that the punishment will be given at a level lower than may be necessary to achieve a lasting solution.

From the human's perspective, there may be a perception that the punishment has worked. The suppression of the response – the fearful dog's body language – is incorrectly interpreted as a fix to the situation. So, when the fearful behaviour re-emerges, or is demonstrated in a new way, the owner returns to their choice of punishment. Only this time, the intensity increases in the belief that the former application was not sufficiently punishing to put an end to the behaviour.

Many clients that I see have gone through several rounds of using punishment at ever-increasing intensities before they seek help. Often, they have grown deeply concerned with the approach they have been advised to use and felt unable to further escalate the punishment due to the distress that their dog is experiencing.

Thankfully, that realisation provides the opportunity to show them that there are other options.

FLOODING

Flooding is a technique that came across to the animal behaviour world after being utilised within human psychotherapy. The aim of flooding is to help an individual overcome their phobic responses. Unfortunately, it is a technique that is often promoted as a means of resolving behavioural issues in dogs.

In the mid-1960s, a psychologist called Thomas Stampfl pioneered a technique, which he called 'implosion therapy'. He found that when phobic patients were bombarded for six to nine hours with descriptions of their fears, they lost their fear of those situations.

Dr. Zev Wanderer, a former professor of psychology at UCLA, refined this research by focusing on the phrases that sparked the most intense reactions among patients and, thus, reduced the therapy period to two hours. To increase the effectiveness of the therapy, and also to shorten the time needed, Wanderer then combined the in-office therapy with recordings of the phrases that were most likely to trigger the phobic reactions, which his patients would take home and listen to as homework.

The underlying theory behind flooding is that learning has taken place to establish the fear. Therefore that learning needs to be unlearned by exposure to whatever has caused the fear. Flooding is based in classical conditioning and biological theory. The biology part is the body's response to stress, which is the fight-or-flight response. When we perceive a threat, the body goes into an alarm stage resulting in the heart beating faster, an increase in blood pressure and adrenaline being released into the blood. However, the body can only stay in this alarm stage for a relatively short period of time. After that, the heart rate drops back down to normal, breathing becomes more regular, and adrenaline levels reduce.

As a result, the person with the phobia discovers that they are no longer panicking, even though they are still being exposed to the very thing that they fear. Now they learn to relax and associate the feared object with their newly learnt, neutral emotion.

Most people with a phobia will avoid any situation that causes them to confront that fear. This avoidance does provide short-term relief from the fear, but it keeps the fear alive, and it encourages avoidance behaviour. Exposure therapy, such as flooding, aims to reduce the irrational feelings by safely exposing the person to different aspects of their fear.

For example, flooding would involve placing a person with a phobia of spiders in a room with a tarantula and then locking the door until they stopped showing fearful responses. The theory being that the individual has now learnt that nothing has happened to them when placed in close proximity to the spider and, as such, they have now developed a new association.

For people, flooding can also be used through providing 'imaginal exposure'. This means that rather than being placed in a room with a spider, the person is asked to imagine being in that situation. This allows for a gradual introduction of the fear rather than implosion first used by Stampfl.

EXTINCTION

Extinction also plays a part in the flooding process. This refers to the gradual weakening of a conditioned response that results in the behaviour decreasing or disappearing. So, that means when extinction is applied, the conditioned behaviour eventually stops. In most cases, this is used when attempting to stop an undesirable behaviour. For example, if a dog is jumping up at you to get attention, you would not react when his feet are off the floor. Over time the dog will learn that he no longer receives the attention he had anticipated, as a consequence of his behaviour, and so he stops jumping up.

We can also consider extinction towards responses that are not under the dog's control. For example, Pavlov found that when his salivating dogs no longer received food when the tone was heard, the salivating eventually stopped; the tone no longer predicted being presented with food.

So let us think about our fearful dogs, and how extinction may take place. Imagine a dog who is out on a walk and is suddenly startled when he turns a corner and comes face-to face with another dog. The startle response causes both dogs to bark at each other. Now whenever the dog is out on a walk and approaches a corner, he begins to show signs of fear. However over a period of time, and with no further confrontations with other dogs as he turns a corner, the fear begins to subside and eventually becomes extinct.

How extinction works is open to some debate. One school of thought states that it involves 'unlearning' the response; another is believes the new response has overcome the previous learning. Either way, there are two other aspects to extinction – and therefore flooding

– that we need to be aware of: firstly the extinction burst and secondly spontaneous recovery.

The extinction burst

An extinction burst is a dramatic increase in the frequency, duration, or intensity of the problem behaviour. This is often presented as –'it's going to get worse before it gets better' – to inform and prepare the client for what seems like a counter intuitive scenario.

If we were to use extinction for our fearful dog as part of the flooding process, we could be inducing more fear during this phase of the protocol. This again illustrates another weakness of the approach in helping a fearful dog. We will not know, when, if, or how often an extinction burst may take place during the flooding process. Nor do we know if our dog will recover and progress to extinction or remain with worsened fears, which have come about because of the extinction burst.

Spontaneous recovery

The return of extinguished behaviour is not unusual, and this can be after a period of time when it was thought the fear had had been successfully extinguished. This can happen when the previous cues for the fear are experienced in new situations. So, for our canine who was worried about a barking dog appearing around the corner, the fear made suddenly reappear if he approaches a corner, which looks similar to the one where the problem first arose. Or, perhaps, it's a dog who looks similar to the one who barked. Each one of these could be a cue which will trigger the fear.

This would seem to support the idea that extinction is about the dog learning a new response to the fear-inducing situation, and that the learning needs to be generalised to a number of different environments before it becomes fully embedded. For our dog, that means lots of street walking, going around corners and having fingers crossed that you don't meet a dog who barks! If we do have a reoccurrence of the fear-inducing set-up during the extinction process, it simply confirms to our poor dog that he was absolutely correct to be fearful of turning a corner.

You can, no doubt, already see some of the gaping holes in applying this technique with a fearful dog rather than with a person. The person has:

– reached a point where they have freely sought help to assist them in overcoming their fears. They have recognised the negative impact it's having on their life, and they are seeking change.
– is informed on what is about to happen. The therapist will have explained the procedure to their client and informed them of how they might feel when the therapy commences and how that leads to the end goal.

– is prepared for the process through learning breathing and relaxation techniques which they can apply when they feel fearful.
– can ask for the process to stop if they feel so overwhelmed that they cannot cope.

RISKS OF USING FLOODING WITH FEARFUL DOGS

Where we realise the importance of providing choice for our dogs, flooding would seem to be at the very opposite end of the spectrum that we are aiming for. It has been suggested that flooding is a suitable technique for very mild fearful responses. However, introducing a mildly fearful dog to the very thing that evokes his fear, may cause it to escalate rather than decline. In addition, you won't know if this will be the outcome of this 'sink or swim' technique until you give it a go.

In a world where we have other choices to help our dogs overcome a fear, it would seem to be both callous and foolhardy to choose flooding when we have so little insight into how our dogs will respond.

FLOODING AND THE RESCUE DOG

Many dogs in a rescue environment can find themselves plunged into a flooding scenario like no other. We know that there are times when this cannot be avoided. For example, it's generally safer for the dog to be in a kennel than out on the street, and many dogs do quickly adapt to their new living environment.

The gregarious, outgoing dog may adjust to the busy situation, with lots of people and other dogs coming and going, with few outward signs of distress. However, the fearful dog is likely to find the intensity of the environment in all its forms, sights, sounds, smells, and physicality to be so over-their-comfort threshold that flooding will be taking place constantly.

There can be an assumption that the dog will go through the extinction process and the kennel environment is no longer a place where he is fearful. That is certainly the case for many dogs who come into rescue and, after a few days of uncertainty, they settle into the new routine. But for some dogs, extinction doesn't happen. They remain in a persistent state of overwhelming fear, which doesn't subside over weeks, months or even years.

For these dogs, our best intentions to 'reassure' them that we humans are nothing to be worried about, can result in an intensified flooding experience. Trying to feed by hand, or to have someone sitting in the kennel, puts the dog in a situation where he cannot escape. Where fostering or relocation to a quiet, less frantic environment is not possible, the Targeted Approach Protocol (TAP) could be a good option. *For more information on this approach for extremely fearful dogs see Chapter Nine.*

I often find that when clients tell me that they have used punishment or flooding, it is because other techniques "didn't work".

When I begin to dig deeper to understand why they have been unsuccessful with a technique such as desensitisation or counter conditioning, it usually comes down to one of two reasons:

Firstly, there has been an expectation of a rapid progression through the process, without assessment of whether the dog was ready to move to the next stage. As a result, the dog has not been prepared for the increase in criteria and the fear has re-emerged.

Secondly, there has been a belief that the fearful responses were under the control of their dog, i.e. he could decide to stop barking or stop shaking when in the presence of the scary thing.

The decision not to inhibit his fearful behaviour has, then, resulted in the use of punishment. In the owner's mind, the dog was in the wrong; they have failed to appreciate that their own lack of knowledge was the limiting factor.

Rarely does an owner want to cause their dog additional suffering but, as you can see, a lack of understanding can result in this being the outcome for the fearful dog.

Owners: I am delighted that you are here! It means that you are developing the knowledge and understanding to prevent your dog from experiencing additional fear from inappropriate techniques.

Behaviourists: it's so important for clients to understand the very real risks that come from using 'don't go there' techniques. The fact that clients are prepared to work with you means that their dogs have a great opportunity to become less fearful and more confident.

ABOUT GALGOS DEL SOL (GDS)

In 2007, Tina Solera, her husband, and two young children moved to Spain to escape the infamous British weather.

Having travelled extensively to explore location options, the Soleras chose Spain as the place to raise their children, with the climate suited to their sporting interests. Little did Tina realise, on moving to Spain, that she would make a decision that would change her life forever. In addition, she changed the lives of thousands of dogs desperately in need of help.

Always an animal lover, Tina could not tolerate the treatment of the Spanish Galgos, a traditional hunting dog breed, and decided to devote herself to their rescue, rehabilitation and rehoming.

The Galgos, with their indomitable spirits, needle-noses and spider-legs, completely captured her heart. One Galgo rescued gave way to another, and another, until it became clear that the Solera household was vastly undersized for the number of dogs that needed help. Murcia, the area in which the Soleras reside, is a prolific hunting ground making the demands on the rescue organisation – Galgos de Sol – relentless.

Never one to turn her back on a dog in need, Tina's commitment is evident by the thousands that she has rehomed in Europe and North America. In addition to her rescue efforts, Tina has also generated public awareness programmes, including a billboard series, as well as initiating an education programme in local schools to promote the care of and respect for hunting dogs. Organisations of this scope cannot function without physical and monetary support; Tina is extremely grateful to devoted friends who tirelessly partner with her to save the Galgos and promote their cause.

Thanks to the generosity and support of their donors, the Galgos del Sol Education and Rescue Centre is fully functional and growing!

After years of keeping the dogs in three different locations at one time, they are now housed in one protected and legally approved facility. The 200-plus dogs reside in two kennel blocks with indoor/outdoor access and piped-in music; there are also exercise areas, a sensory walk for stimulation and an agility area for training. There is a residence for the full-time on-site volunteers, an education building for the school-age community programmes, a quarantine block with six kennels, a free standing kitchen and a puppy block. The GDS local and international volunteer programme has proved a great success for socialising the dogs. GDS strives to provide the very best for the dogs while they are waiting to be adopted into their forever homes.

WHAT IS A GALGO?

The Galgo Español or Spanish Greyhound is an ancient breed and is a member of the sighthound family. Despite being called a 'Greyhound', the Spanish Galgo is not closely related to the English or Irish Greyhound, as the lineage of the two breeds are different.

In ancient times the Galgo was a prized possession, but currently, they have become disposable 'hunting tools'. GDS believes Galgos are an integral part of Spanish legacy and deserve to be returned to a place of respect.

Galgos can be either smooth or rough-coated and come in a variety of colours; their coat may be one solid colour, brindle, or two colours in combination. They are similar in appearance to racing Greyhounds but are distinctly different in their conformation. Galgos have a leaner musculature, more characteristic of an endurance runner than the 'sprinter's' build of the English/Irish racing Greyhound. They are long, lean, elegant dogs; in fact, it's hard to describe them without over-using the word 'long'; they have long backs, long tails and long, streamlined heads with almond-shaped eyes.

Galgos have a similar nature to Greyhounds; many are calm, usually quiet, gentle and laid back. They are, however, curious, and many are jumpers — baby gates and 1.2 m (4 ft) fences are not an obstacle to them. Described as 65km (40mph) couch-potatoes, they are content to sleep their day away and they are happy with a couple of short walks per day, but they can also make excellent jogging companions. Many Galgos live with cats, and other small animals without a problem, while others, given careful introductions, can be trained to do so once they have learned the appropriate boundaries.

Galgos are widely used by hunters in the rural areas of Spain for both hunting and hare coursing staged for betting. They are considered disposable, and when the short hunting season ends each year, tens of thousands are abandoned or brutally killed by their owners to whom they are no longer of use.

Some of the GDS Galgos have been saved from perreras (killing stations) where their lives were due to be ended. Others that were abandoned had been living rough, and scavenging to survive, until caught by volunteers who themselves often face hostility from their fellow countrymen for showing concern for a breed deemed worthless.

THE GDS VOLUNTEER PROGRAMME

A hard-working core team of staff ensure that all the needs of every dog are met. However, with the help of volunteers, the dogs can receive even more one-on-one time with increased opportunities to discover that humans can be the source of kindness, and provide a great supply of treats!

For more information on rehoming, sponsorship opportunities and the volunteer programme, take a look at the Galgos del Sol website: *http://www.galgosdelsol.org*.

For daily updates on the dogs at the centre, check out the Galgos del Sol Facebook page.